PE2theMAX

Maximize Skills, Participation, Teamwork, and Fun

J.D. Hughes

Human Kinetics

Library of Congress Cataloging-in-Publication Data

Hughes, J.D., 1972-
    PE2themax : maximize skills, participation, teamwork, and fun / J.D.
Hughes.
        p. cm.
    Includes bibliographical references.
    ISBN 0-7360-5635-1 (soft cover)
    1. Physical education for children.   2. Games.   I. Title.
    GV443.H75   2005
    372.86--dc22   2005000957

ISBN-10: 0-7360-5635-1
ISBN-13: 978-0-7360-5635-9

The Web addresses cited in this text were current as of 12/20/2004, unless otherwise noted.

Acquisitions Editor: Scott Wikgren; **Developmental Editor:** Melissa Feld; **Assistant Editors:** Derek Campbell, Ragen E. Sanner, and Ann M. Augspurger; **Copyeditor:** Alisha Jeddeloh; **Proofreader:** Sue Fetters; **Permission Manager:** Dalene Reeder; **Graphic Designer:** Fred Starbird; **Graphic Artist:** Yvonne Griffith; **Photo Manager:** Kelly J. Huff; **Cover Designer:** Keith Blomberg; **Illustrator (cover):** Keith Blomberg; **Art Manager:** Kelly Hendren; **Illustrator:** Argosy; **Printer:** Versa Press

On the cover: In the game Nuclear Reaction (see pages 59-62), students work together to form a complete molecule.

Printed in the United States of America   10   9   8   7   6   5

Human Kinetics
Web site: www.HumanKinetics.com

United States: Human Kinetics, P.O. Box 5076, Champaign, IL 61825-5076
800-747-4457
e-mail: humank@hkusa.com

Canada: Human Kinetics, 475 Devonshire Road, Unit 100, Windsor, ON N8Y 2L5
800-465-7301 (in Canada only)
e-mail: info@hkcanada.com

Europe: Human Kinetics, 107 Bradford Road, Stanningley
Leeds LS28 6AT, United Kingdom
+44 (0) 113 255 5665
e-mail: hk@hkeurope.com

Australia: Human Kinetics, 57A Price Avenue, Lower Mitcham, South Australia 5062
08 8372 0999
e-mail: info@hkaustralia.com

New Zealand: Human Kinetics, Division of Sports Distributors NZ Ltd.
P.O. Box 300 226 Albany, North Shore City, Auckland
0064 9 448 1207
e-mail: info@humankinetics.co.nz

I dedicate this book to the God-given girls in my life, my wife Beth and daughters Janie and Josie. Thank you for the hugs, kisses, and open arms that I come home to each day.

To all physical education specialists who strive to improve themselves and challenge their students despite budget cuts, poor schedules, oversized classes, and lack of support. You are truly heroes. May you continue to make a difference in the lives of our young people.

With my deepest love and respect,
J.D. Hughes

Contents

Preface

Are you ready to be blown away by a new wave of physical education games? If so, then welcome to *PE2theMax,* a book of exciting games that goes hand in hand with a quality physical education program and the New PE philosophy that's sweeping the nation. It is my desire to help you look at games with a new perspective and realize the dynamic role games can play in physical education.

Quality physical education programs provide learning experiences that meet children's developmental needs, which in turn improves mental alertness, academic performance, and readiness and enthusiasm for learning (NASPE 2004). Young (2003) purports that such a program provides a supportive environment in which students learn positive competition, respect for others, and the satisfaction of doing their best.

The idea of New PE is to get away from the jock culture, which emphasizes being the fastest, strongest, and most athletic, and start all kids on the road to lifelong fitness (Lawler 2002). New PE advocates say it's time to scrap the physical education programs most baby boomers experienced. They believe that team sports put many children in situations where they fail in public and thus withdraw from the activity, increasing their risk not only for obesity but also heart disease, the United States' number one cause of death (Weir 2000). The New PE philosophy emphasizes programs that include a variety of enjoyable, inclusive physical activities designed to build self-confidence and promote cooperation, fair play, and responsible participation while encouraging lifetime fitness.

Despite the National Association of Sport and Physical Education's (NASPE) emphasis on quality physical education and the New PE philosophy, there are still alarming rates of inactivity and obesity in today's young people. The surge in childhood obesity among the fast-food generation indicates they could reach middle age with the weakest hearts in the nation's history, setting off a health care disaster (Weir 2000). The relentless lure of television, computers, and video games is starting to overwhelm children.

With the emergence of the New PE philosophy, physical education is clearly evolving, but the most important ingredient to solving the problem of childhood obesity is fun. Chen and Darst (1999) attribute students' low motivation for learning physical skills to a lack of interesting skills to learn. Why do kids enjoy computer and video games? They're *fun.* Ask any kid what her favorite sport, hobby, or game is, followed by the question "Why is it your favorite?" and the most likely response is "Because it's fun." Some experts believe that kids choose whether they will be active or not. But George Graham, Penn State University health and physical education professor, commented that it's when children don't have much of a chance to participate, or when they don't have a lot of fun, they shut down (Weir 2000).

This ideology goes hand in hand with the "games for understanding" approach to PE because what is meaningful to the students is playing the game, not practicing the skills. Although games should build physical fitness and teach skills, fun should be their focus. A well-planned lesson or game that incorporates all the components of a quality physical education program is worthless if a child is not having fun. Classes should be action packed, with lots of choices, equipment, and opportunities for students of all skill levels to successfully meet challenges. It is crucial, especially during the elementary and middle school years, that we never place students in situations where they are likely to fail or feel embarrassed, thus contributing to a negative outlook on physical activity. It is time that we move from comfortable, familiar, and functional physical education to movement education that is rich with fun, challenging, and dynamic experiences.

I focused on creating inclusive, developmentally appropriate games that are fun without sacrificing the integrity of the components of a quality physical education program and the New PE philosophy. I tried to create fun, movement-based, skill-based games that promote communication, cooperation, and personal responsibility and help children learn to apply critical-thinking and problem-solving skills, crucial life skills that allow us to think for ourselves and be productive human beings. Incorporating these life skills into game situations provides children with practical, hands-on approaches to practicing and learning these life skills.

It is my pleasure to present to you *PE2theMax: Maximize Skills, Participation, Teamwork, and Fun.* This book is a guide to enhancing any physical education program. Although equipment needs for the games are based on large classes, the games are designed for any class size. I've used large class sizes as examples because it is easy adapt a game to meet the needs of smaller classes by simply not using as much equipment. This is what makes this book different—most games are designed for smaller classes, making them nearly impossible to use with larger classes. Because they are not designed to get everyone in a larger class involved, many students spend time sitting out. This resource provides invigorating and challenging activities for classes of all sizes, resulting in minimal discipline problems and maximal participation.

Physical education is one of the best ways to teach proficiency in a wide array of movement concepts and motor skills. But most importantly, physical education provides the perfect place to teach life, social, and critical-thinking skills. Games should go beyond rote memorization of skills to problems that require students to brainstorm, collaborate, put into action, and evaluate strategies. Maina, Griffin, and McCurdy (2002) have found that integrating critical thinking into children's learning experiences may improve their ability to think for themselves and prepare them for solving problems throughout their lifetime. I challenge you to take advantage of opportunities to relate the game's challenges to real-life situations that students may encounter one day.

All games and activities are classroom-tested and have been used successfully with children ages 4 to 13. They maximize participation and ensure that every child is provided with numerous opportunities for success while learning basic fitness- and sport-related skills. I have placed special emphasis on experiences that encourage teamwork and improve self-esteem, initiative, decision making, and creative thinking. These values are instilled through motivating, challenging games and activities that will have all children wanting more.

These coeducational units and games provide flexibility in that educators can easily combine them with already-established units and modify them to best meet program needs. The games contain easy-to-read illustrations and diagrams to aid in class setup. Although most lessons and games use standard physical education equipment, additional equipment may be appropriate.

Let *PE2theMax* guide you toward greater success in your physical education program and, most important, students having lots of fun in the gym. Now let's play!

Acknowledgments

Jesus, lover of my soul, thank you for taking my place on the cross. Without you, there is no hope. Thank you for filling the void in my life and giving me joy.

This book would not have been possible without the wonderful children of Mirror Lake and Arbor Station Elementary Schools, who endured the sometimes exhausting process of creating these unique games. I realized this on the day one child asked, "Are we going to be your lab rats today?" Their willingness and patience were invaluable.

A special thanks to the following contributors who, through their ideas, were instrumental in the creation of this book:

Shannon "Daniel" Boone
Jill "Grammar Geek" Zehr
Raymond "Butch" Soles
Tony "T-Bone" Harris
Terence "Wannabe" Choates
All of the children at Mirror Lake
    and Arbor Station Elementary Schools

How to Use This Book

PE2theMax contains innovative physical education games for elementary and middle school classes with as few as 16 students and as many as 80. This section will familiarize you with the organizational format of each game. You will also find tips for using the game finder, a quick reference tool designed to help you quickly access game information as you plan lessons.

Game Organization

- Grade level: Age group the game works best with.
- Objective: Game's purpose and some or all of the skills it reinforces. See the game finder for a complete list of skills reinforced.
- Equipment: Equipment needed to meet the game's objective. Please note that the amount of necessary equipment will vary according to class size. For example, the number of items listed for each piece of equipment might be based on a class of 48 students with 6 players per team. For smaller or larger classes, simply provide the amount of equipment needed for the number of teams.
- The equipment is only recommended. You might decide a game would benefit from adding, subtracting, or completely eliminating some of the recommended equipment. Also, you can substitute similar pieces of equipment. For example, instead of using 28-inch traffic cones as targets, markers, and dividers, you can use smaller cones, poly spots, or any other suitable item.
- Diagrams and figures: Diagrams of the game's setup illustrate approximately where to place equipment. Due to facility or space limitations and safety, you may need to adapt the setup. Figures are included to help you visualize part of the activity.
- Scenario: Sequence of events or story to help get imaginations flowing and prepare students for the exciting game ahead. Not all games have a scenario.
- Procedure: Recommended series of steps for game setup and preparation. Pay close attention to the object of the game, how to begin, and special notes and options.
- Rules and safety: Overview of rules that help maintain a safe environment.
- Variations: Possible modifications to enhance or alter each game's outcome. The variations listed are not exhaustive—make creative changes in order to meet your program's needs.

Teaching Tips

- Take advantage of opportunities to relate the game challenge to real-life situations students will encounter one day. The end of a game is often an ideal opportunity for such discussions.
- Unless otherwise indicated, all games are designed to be played in a gym or open space. You can modify any game or activity by varying equipment or play-area dimensions to meet your program's goals.
- The systems for equipment setup and dispersion, the signals for starting and stopping games, and the methods for dealing with behavior problems are necessary time-management components that help ensure the overall success of each game.

- Consider the time of year, season, and weather conditions when determining game compatibility, especially when the gym is not the ideal place for the activity.

- Try the following grouping methods, which give students the responsibility of choosing groups. If problems arise in a group, remind students that they chose their group and are responsible for following class rules and working together.

  - Instruct students to go to any group, put on a colored jersey, and wait for further instructions. When playing The Great Escape, for example, the jerseys for two groups are put in designated places before classes arrive. Have students locate and wear whatever color jerseys are available. This works well for many of the games in this book.

  - Perform a 10-second countdown at the beginning of class to quickly group students or to have them find a space on the floor. For example, say "groups of four" and begin the 10-second countdown. During the countdown, students choose their own groups. After the countdown, they come to you so you can instruct them to go to a particular area of the gym.

  - Use a whistle blow. Students quickly learn how to react to this great nonverbal cue. Students get into groups based on how many times the whistle blows. For example, say you give six short, loud whistle blows, and then repeat the six short, loud whistle blows, giving the signal twice in case students were not listening the first time. Students react quickly by forming groups of six.

- For additional resources, see Suggested Readings and References on page 100.

Game-Finder Organization

- Grade level: Age groups the game works best with.

- Unit wrap-up: Suggestions for ways to use the game as a culminating game or finale of particular units or lessons. For example, Supremacy would be an excellent culminating game of a hockey unit.

- Skills reinforced: List of skills that each game reinforces.

- Number of players: Suggested number of participants.

- Equipment: Items that each game requires.

- Time: Approximate amount of time needed to play a round or complete game. Game times will vary according to class size, age range, and physical and mental development.

- Page number: Location of the game in this book.

Game Finder

Game	Grade level	Unit wrap-up	Skills reinforced	# of players	Equipment	Time	Page #
Ballistic	2-8	Ball manipulation Bowling Target practice	Aiming for accuracy Bowling Scooters Strategizing Teamwork Throwing	16-80	Basketball goals Containers for storing yarn balls Gator Skin balls Jerseys (optional) Scooters Traffic cones Trash cans or barrels Yarn balls or noodle pieces	20-45 minutes	1
Bewildered	2-8	Cooperatives Ball manipulation Relationships with objects and people	Catching Communication Critical thinking Listening Problem solving Strategizing Teamwork Throwing	14-84	Beach balls Hula hoops Noodles Phase Challenges handout	20-30 minutes	4
Boo-Yah	3-8	Ball manipulation Bowling Scooters Target practice	Aiming for accuracy Bowling Problem solving Strategizing Teamwork Throwing	16-80	Basketball goals Containers for storing yarn balls Gator Skin balls or volleyball trainers Jerseys (optional) Scooters Storage containers Tennis balls Traffic cones Yarn balls	20-45 minutes	8
Bounce Brigade	2-8	Ball manipulation Cooperatives Relationships with objects and people Spatial awareness Target practice	Aiming for accuracy Catching Communication Eye–hand coordination Patience Strategizing Teamwork Throwing	16-80	5-gallon buckets Cans or plastic buckets Hula hoops Ricochet balls (optional) Wiffle or tennis balls	20-30 minutes	12
Bowl-a-Hula	K-8	Hula hoop manipulatives Relationships with objects and people Spatial awareness Traveling	Aiming for accuracy Chasing, fleeing, dodging Communication Eye–hand coordination Hula hooping Hula jumping Teamwork	16-80	Gator Skin or playground balls Hula hoops Jerseys (optional)	15-45 minutes	15

Game	Grade level	Unit wrap-up	Skills reinforced	# of players	Equipment	Time	Page #
Bowling Blitz	K-3	Ball manipulation Relationships with objects and people	Aiming for accuracy Bowling Defense	16-80	Bowling pins Gator Skin balls Traffic cones	15-45 minutes	19
BRYG It On	K-6	Relationships with objects and people Spatial awareness Traveling	Chasing, fleeing, dodging Teamwork	16-80	Hula hoops Sonic Flag-A-Tag belts	15-45 minutes	22
Building Blocks	2-8	Cooperatives Fitness concepts Traveling	Communication Critical thinking Problem solving Teamwork	16-80	Hula hoops Noodle pieces Storage containers Yardstick	30-45 minutes	25
C.H.A.O.S.	K-8	Cooperatives Traveling	Chasing, fleeing, dodging Scooters Strategizing Teamwork	16-80	Hula hoops Jerseys Noodles Scooters 4 of each of the following items (different items may be substituted): balloons, bean-bags, birdees, bowling pins, checkers, flags, Gator Skin balls, lummi sticks, noodle pieces, poly spots, pucks, scarves, tennis balls, Wiffle balls, yarn balls	20-30 minutes	29
Crocodile Mile	K-8	Relationships with objects and people Spatial awareness Traveling	Chasing, fleeing, dodging Communication Jumping Strategizing Teamwork	16-80	5-gallon buckets (optional) Hula hoops Poly spots Scooters Traffic Cones Yarn balls or noodle pieces	15-45 minutes	32
Empire Mania	2-8	Cooperatives Ball manipulation Relationships with objects and people Spatial awareness Target practice Traveling	Adaptability Catching Eye–hand coordination Problem solving Spontaneity Teamwork Throwing	16-80	Gator Skin balls Jerseys	15-45 minutes	35

Game	Grade level	Unit wrap-up	Skills reinforced	# of players	Equipment	Time	Page #
Finesse	K-8	Bowling Effort Frisbee Noodles	Aiming for accuracy Bowling Strategizing Teamwork Throwing	16-80	Foam or indoor Frisbees Hula hoops Gator Skin balls Jerseys Noodles Poly spots Scooters Trash cans	20-45 minutes	38
Flag 'Em Down	2-8	Cooperatives Relationships with objects and people	Adaptability Chasing, fleeing, dodging Communication Eye–hand coordination Strategizing Teamwork	16-80	5-gallon buckets Hula hoops Sonic Flag-A-Tag belts	30-45 minutes	41
The Great Escape	K-8	Ball manipulation Scooters Relationships with objects and people	Aiming for accuracy Problem solving Rolling and bowling Strategizing Teamwork Throwing	16-80	Basketball goals Bowling pins Containers Gator Skin balls Jerseys (optional) Scooters Traffic cones Wiffle, tennis, or hockey balls	15-25 minutes	44
H₂O No!	2-8	Cooperatives Noodles Relationships with objects and people	Catching Communication Critical thinking Eye–hand coordination Problem solving Strategizing Teamwork	16-80	5-gallon buckets Frisbees Gator Skin balls Hockey sticks Hula hoops Jerseys (optional) Noodles Storage containers	30-45 minutes	47
Head Honcho II	2-8	Relationships with objects and people	Addition Communication Honorable sporting behavior Strategizing	16-80	25-50 blindfolds, lummi sticks, or other items 5-gallon buckets 50-100 scarves, checkers, or other items 100-200 tongue depressors or Popsicle sticks Floor tape (optional) Hula hoops, carpet squares, or large poly spots	15-45 minutes	51

Game	Grade level	Unit wrap-up	Skills reinforced	# of players	Equipment	Time	Page #
Hideout	K-5	Relationships with objects and people	Adaptability Chasing, fleeing, dodging Defense Strategizing Teamwork	16-80	Gymnastic mats Hula hoops Lummi sticks Noodles cut in half Sonic Flag-A-Tag belts Traffic cones	15-45 minutes	54
Med Alert	3-8	Ball manipulation Cooperatives Effort Relationships with objects and people	Communication Critical thinking Eye–hand coordination Problem solving Strategizing Teamwork	16-80	5-gallon buckets Frisbees Hula hoops Jerseys (optional) Noodles cut in half Traffic cones Wiffle, tennis, or hockey balls	30-45 minutes	56
Nuclear Reaction	K-8	Ball manipulation Cooperatives Effort Relationships with objects and people	Aiming for accuracy Bowling Communication Problem solving Strategizing Teamwork	16-60	Gator Skin balls Hula hoops Jerseys Noodles Traffic cones	10-15 minutes	59
Operation "Space Junkyard"	K-8	Cooperatives Relationships with objects and people	Communication Critical thinking Problem solving Strategizing Teamwork	16-80	Blindfolds Gator Skin balls Hockey sticks Hula hoops Poly spots Scooters Trophy	30-45 minutes	63
Pacemaker	2-8	Cooperatives Fitness concepts Relationships with objects and people Traveling	Communication Teamwork	16-80	5-gallon buckets 1000 tongue depressors or Popsicle sticks Hula hoops or poly spots Pacemaker Progressions list Traffic cones (optional)	20-45 minutes	66
Pindemonium	2-8	Frisbees Target practice	Aiming for accuracy Bowling Defense Throwing	16-80	Basketball goals Bowling pins Gator Skin balls Indoor Frisbees (optional) Jerseys Trash cans	20-45 minutes	70
Scooter Blitz	K-6	Ball manipulation Relationships with objects and people	Aiming for accuracy Bowling Defense Offense Scooters Strategizing Teamwork Throwing	16-80	Bowling pins Gator Skin balls Jerseys (optional) Scooters Traffic cones	15-20 minutes	72

Game	Grade level	Unit wrap-up	Skills reinforced	# of players	Equipment	Time	Page #
Shockey	2-8	Ball manipulation Cooperatives Hockey Long-handled implements Relationships with objects and people	Adaptability Aiming for accuracy Chasing, fleeing, dodging Communication Critical thinking Defense Offense Problem solving Strategizing Teamwork	16-80	Gator Skin balls Hockey sticks Jerseys Lummi sticks Trash cans, barrels, or boxes	20-45 minutes	74
Super Bowl	K-8	Ball manipulation Relationships with objects and people	Aiming for accuracy Bowling Defense Offense	16-80	Bowling pins Gator Skin balls Jerseys (optional) Tennis balls Traffic cones	15-20 minutes	77
Supremacy	2-8	Ball manipulation Hockey Long-handled implements Relationships with objects and people	Aiming for accuracy Bowling Defense Offense Teamwork	16-80	5-gallon buckets Bowling pins Gator Skin balls Hockey sticks Jerseys Tennis balls Traffic cones Yarn balls	20-45 minutes	80
Under Siege	2-8	Relationships with objects and people Traveling	Defense Eye–hand coordination Offense Strategizing Teamwork	16-80	Gator Skin balls Hula hoops Sonic Flag-A-Tag belts	10-45 minutes	84
Well Designed	3-8	Ball manipulation Basketball Cooperatives Jump rope Relationships with objects and people Scooters	Communication Memorization Strategizing Teamwork	16-80	Badminton rackets Basketball Bowling pins Frisbees Hockey sticks Hula hoop Jump ropes Laminated Diagram 1 and 2 Lummi stick Noodles Pencils Playground ball Poly spots Scooter boards Scooters Traffic cones Well Designed Fitness Checklist Yarn balls	25-45 minutes	87

Game	Grade level	Unit wrap-up	Skills reinforced	# of players	Equipment	Time	Page #
Wheel 'n Deal	1-8	Cooperatives Relationships with objects and people	Communication Strategizing Teamwork	16-80	Hula hoops 13 of each of the following items (different items may be substituted): red and black checkers, scarves, green and blue lummi sticks, birdies, Wiffle balls, orange and purple beanbags, yellow and blue yarn balls, blindfolds, foam Frisbees	10-15 minutes	93
Yeah, Baby!	K-8	Ball manipulation Effort Frisbees	Aiming for accuracy Bowling Defense Offense Strategizing Teamwork Throwing	16-80	5-gallon buckets Basketball goals Bowling pins Gator Skin balls Hula hoops Indoor Frisbees Jerseys Traffic cones Wiffle, tennis, or hockey balls	25-45 minutes	97

BALLISTIC

Objective

This game emphasizes teamwork and strategy. The more "ball"istic the students go, the more points they can earn for their team.

Equipment

Needs are based on a class of 20 to 80 students.

- ▶ Basketball goals set 8 feet high (2)
- ▶ Containers for storing yarn balls (2)
- ▶ Gator Skin balls (50-75; the more the better)
- ▶ Jerseys to designate teams (optional, but recommended)
- ▶ Scooters (16)
- ▶ Traffic cones, 28-inch (8-12)
- ▶ Trash cans or barrels (2)
- ▶ Yarn balls or noodle pieces (at least 150, half in one color and half in another color)

Scenario

The world's elite athletes have been summoned to the remote island of Pandar. Located on Pandar is the famous Coliseum Royale, known for the amazing sporting event of Ballistic Ball. Ballistic Ball challenges even the best athletes because it demands a high degree of target accuracy. The winning team gets to claim the world's ultimate prize—being declared the Ballistic Ball World Champions.

Procedure

Before students arrive, place four traffic cones on their side and eight scooters upside down against each end wall of the gym. Place the containers of yarn balls against the middle of each end wall of the gym. Place the empty barrels diagonal to each other and at opposite ends of the gym. Finally, place 50 to 75 Gator Skin balls in the middle of the gym (see diagram for setup).

The object of the game is to have the most yarn balls when the designated time limit expires. Read the scenario to the class. Divide the class into two teams and send teams to opposite ends of the gym to sit down and await further instructions.

Each team must earn ways to go and collect the yarn balls at the opposite end of the gym. Teams race against each other to earn the most points, or yarn balls. The three ways to earn points are as follows:

1. Any player who rolls or throws a Gator Skin ball so that it lands on top of a scooter at the opposite end of the gym may retrieve that scooter. The players who earn a scooter may ride their scooter to collect 1 yarn ball at a time and add it to their team's trash can. Players with a scooter may ride it until the game is over, trade responsibilities with other teammates, or set the scooter against a sidewall to be used by anyone who wants to use it.

2. Any player who shoots or throws a ball so that it goes into the opposing team's basketball goal may walk across the midline and gather 5 yarn balls to add to their team's trash can.

3. Any player who rolls or throws a ball so that it lands inside a cone may immediately walk across the midline, retrieve the ball from the cone, and then gather 10 yarn balls and add them to their team's trash can.

Players may also steal the opponent's points by attempting to throw the balls into the opponent's barrel of points. Each score allows the throwing player to steal 2 different colored yarn balls from the opposing team's trash can to be returned to the original storage container.

The first team to collect all of the yarn balls or to collect the most yarn balls when the 20- to 30-minute time limit has expired is the winner for that round. Clean up and start a new round.

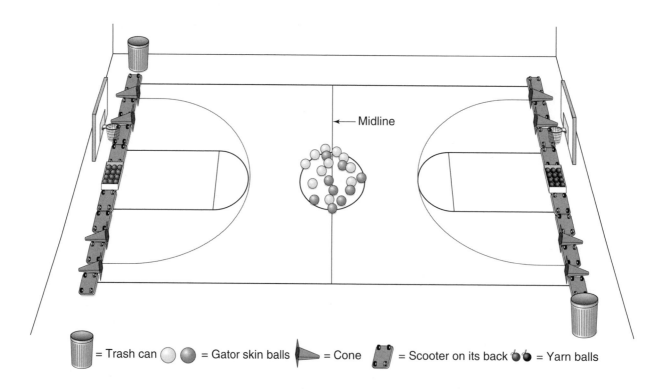

= Trash can   = Gator skin balls   = Cone   = Scooter on its back   = Yarn balls

Rules and Safety

1. Players may only cross the midline if they have successfully achieved one of the four ways to gain points. If players earn the right to steal yarn balls from the opposing team and that team has not yet collected many yarn balls, the players steal whatever balls are available.

2. Players may only collect and throw one Gator Skin ball at a time. Remind players to watch the balls until they stop or land because all thrown or rolled balls have the potential to score points.

3. Players with scooters may take only one yarn ball at a time and must return to their team's barrel before going to get another point. Players may go forward or backward but must remain seated on their bottom. Players on scooters may also assist their team by returning Gator Skin balls to their team's side.

4. Players who earn scooters may switch with any teammate at any time or park the scooter. Any player can claim a scooter if a ball is resting on top of it and nobody has claimed it.

5. Defense of targets is not allowed.

6. Any player who scores a ball into a cone must retrieve the thrown ball before collecting the 10 yarn balls.

7. Taking more than the allotted yarn balls for a given task will result in points being deducted. The teacher determines the number of points to be taken away.

8. Players who earn points must go and personally collect the earned points.

9. Players who make a score in the opposing team's trash can must return all yarn balls they collected to the original container and not their team's trash can.

Variations

1. Allow an unlimited number of defenders to guard the targets. Or, designate 2, 3, or 4 defenders per team (different colored jerseys will be necessary to distinguish defenders).

2. Increase or decrease equipment based on class needs or size.

3. Substitute large trash cans if basketball goals are too high or too hard to score in. Place trash cans underneath the basketball goals or at a comparable distance.

4. Allow more or fewer yarn balls to be taken for each score.

BEWILDERED

Objective

This game allows students to collaborate and use critical thinking to determine the best strategies for transferring the beach balls.

Equipment

Needs are based on a class of 56 students (8 teams of 7 players).

- Beach balls, 20-inch or smaller (24)
- Hula hoops (16 in 8 different colors; for example, 2 blue, 2 red, 2 yellow, and so on)
- Noodles (24)
- Phase Challenges handout (8 copies), page 7

Procedure

Before students arrive, place eight hula hoops flat on the floor against the wall at one end of the gym and place the like-color hoops directly opposite, laid flat against the wall at the other end of the gym. At one end of the gym, place three beach balls and three noodles inside each hula hoop (see diagram for setup).

The object of the game is for each team to successfully complete three challenging phases. Teams race against each other to see who can complete the three phases the fastest (see page 6 for examples of how to complete each phase and page 7 for the phase challenges handout). No positions will be assigned. Players are responsible for determining strategies and choosing what role they want to play.

Divide the class into eight teams of seven and send each team to one of the eight hula hoops full of equipment, where students sit down and await further instructions. Instruct all teams to choose one player to be their captain. Each captain then reports to you to get a copy of the phase challenges (see page 7).

Captains read the phase challenges to their team and collaborate with teammates to determine the best strategy to successfully complete phase 1. Each team continues this process until they have completed all three phases. The first team to complete all three phases is the winner of that round. Clean up and start a new round.

It is important for you to walk among the groups and observe for student comprehension. Stop the game and clarify instructions or provide hints when necessary.

Rules and Safety

1. Each team must carefully read and follow the instructions on the Phase Challenges handout.
2. Any strategy is admissible as long as it does not violate any of the rules. The teacher moves around the room and tells teams to start over if they are violating a rule.

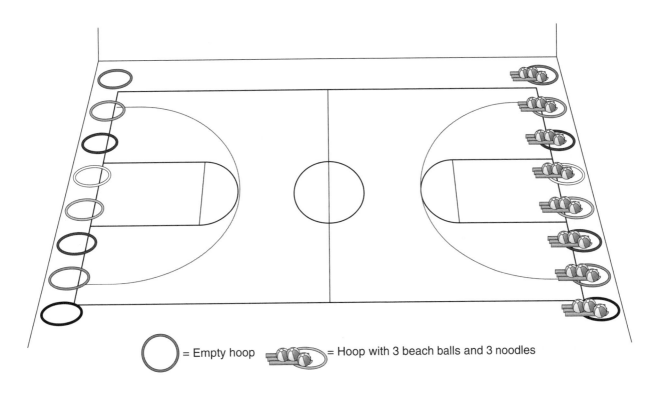

= Empty hoop   = Hoop with 3 beach balls and 3 noodles

3. Everyone must clearly be participating and contributing to each team's overall success. If this is not evident, then the teacher should instruct teams to create a strategy that includes all teammates. Any strategy that involves individuals completing a task by themselves is unacceptable.

4. Teams may not hinder other teams.

Variations

1. Create new phases to be completed. A fourth phase, for example, could include the following:

   a. Transfer each ball back across the gym and place each ball inside your hoop.

   b. All balls must be rolled on the floor, and each ball must be under someone at all times when being advanced toward the hoop.

   c. Start phase 4 over from the beginning if any ball makes contact with a player or is advanced without being under a teammate.

2. Add more beach balls to each team's hoop.

▶ *Phase 1.*

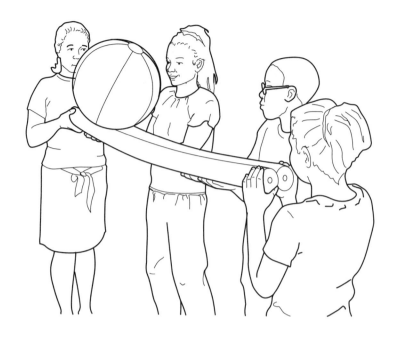

▶ *Phase 2.*

▶ *Phase 3.*

Phase Challenges

Your team has access to three noodles and three beach balls. Noodles may be used to complete each phase. At no time can the noodles be bent or folded! Your challenge for each phase is to transfer and place all three beach balls inside your team's hula hoop located directly across the gym. *Everyone must participate when transferring balls or your team will be asked to start over!* You must stay within the following rules to complete each phase.

Phase 1

 a. Transfer each ball to your hoop at the opposite end of the gym without any ball touching the floor. All balls must be placed inside the hula hoop.
 b. You may not carry or roll the balls, and you may not advance toward a hoop while in possession of a ball. However, human contact can be made with the balls.
 c. Return all beach balls and start phase 1 over from the beginning if a player advances with a ball or any ball makes contact with the floor before being placed inside the hula hoop.

Phase 2

 a. Transfer each ball back across the gym, one at a time, and place each ball inside your hoop.
 b. Each ball must be carried and may not touch the floor. No form of human contact can be made with the balls at any time.
 c. Return all beach balls and start phase 2 over from the beginning if human contact is made with a ball or any ball touches the floor before or after being placed inside the hula hoop.

Phase 3

 a. Transfer each ball back across the gym and place each ball inside your hoop.
 b. All balls must be rolled from hoop to hoop without any ball touching the floor. Human contact can be made with the balls with any body part *except the hands and arms.* Balls may not be carried.
 c. Return all beach balls and start phase 3 over from the beginning if any ball makes contact with anyone's hands or arms or the ball contacts the floor before or after being placed inside the hula hoop.

From *PE2theMax: Maximize Skills, Participation, Teamwork, and Fun* by J.D. Hughes, 2005, Champaign, IL: Human Kinetics.

BOO-YAH

Objective

This is a heart-racing teamwork game where strategy, throwing for accuracy, and problem-solving skills help teams claim Boo-Yah and earn victory.

Equipment

Needs are based on a class of 30 to 80 students.

- Basketball goals at opposite ends of the gym, set 8 feet high (2)
- Containers for yarn balls (4)
- Gator Skin balls or volleyball trainers (50-100)
- Jerseys to distinguish teams (optional)
- Scooters (16)
- Storage containers
- Tennis balls (16)
- Traffic cones, 28-inch (16)
- Yarn balls in two different colors (50-100 of each color)

Scenario

It is the year 3001 and all of the world's natural energy resources have diminished except for one, the precious element of Boo-Yah, found only in the city of Kryptonia. Boo-Yah, although small and hard to locate, is the strongest power source known to humankind. All of the leading world powers are sending their best special agents to Kryptonia to gather as much Boo-Yah as possible.

Procedure

Before classes arrive, place eight traffic cones on each end line and place a tennis ball on top of each cone. Place a scooter behind each traffic cone. Then place both containers of yarn balls at each end of the gym against the wall. Place the empty containers diagonal to each other and at opposite ends of the gym. Finally, place 50 to 100 Gator Skin balls in the middle of the gym (see diagram for setup).

The object of the game is to be the first team to retrieve the most Boo-Yah (yarn balls) from inside the heavily secured electric fence (cones with tennis balls). Divide the class into 2 teams and choose 2 or 3 captains for each team. Instruct students to go to their side of the gym and put on a jersey. Read the scenario to the class.

Each team throws or bowls balls at the opposing team's cones, attempting to destroy the electric fence on the opposite end of the gym (knock the tennis balls off the cones). Each ball that is knocked off of a cone causes a "hole" in the opposing team's electric fence. A hole is any area between a cone without a ball and any other cone that may or may not still have a ball. Each player who destroys part of the electric fence by knocking a ball off a cone must yell "Boo-Yah" to notify everyone that a ball was knocked off a cone. After knocking a ball off, any player destroying the opposing team's electric fence may cross over the midline to the opposing team's side and retrieve the hovercraft (scooter) that is directly behind the cone. For example, if players knock six balls off six cones, they may use the six hovercrafts behind those cones.

Players may then use the hovercrafts to gather Boo-Yah (yarn balls) one at a time from their opponent's container to travel through the damaged areas of the electric fence to bring back to their team's empty container. For example, players on scooters may travel back and forth between any set of cones that has at least one missing ball. Students must realize that the more scooters are used, the more Boo-Yah they can steal. Note: Make sure players on scooters only travel through the holes or damaged areas of the electric fence to collect Boo-Yah and return to their team's container.

Only eight scooters are provided per team so that the majority of players are available to roll and throw balls to destroy the electric fence. It is up to each team to keep track of how many scooters they can use. Players may park the scooters or switch with a teammate if they tire of being on a scooter.

Each team also has a portal (basketball goal) located at the opposite end of the gym. Explain that a portal is a doorway for going back in time. Players who throw balls and make a goal or hit the rim also yell "Boo-Yah" to notify everyone of their accomplishment and then go "back in time" through a portal to repair part of their team's electric fence by setting one ball back on any cone that is missing a ball. Repairing the electric fence slows the opposing team down because they cannot travel between cones that are undamaged. Also, when part of a fence is repaired the opposing team loses the use of one scooter because of the rule that each team may only use one scooter for every ball that is knocked off a cone. A player returning a ball must also retrieve a scooter from the opposing team and return it behind the repaired fence.

It is possible that a team will knock off all of the opposing team's balls. If this occurs, players who were destroying the opposing team's electric fence should focus on scoring goals or hitting the rim to go back in time to repair their own fence. The first team to collect all of the Boo-Yah or to collect the most Boo-Yah in 25-30 minutes will be declared the winner for that round. Clean up and start a new round.

The most important job is in the hands of each team's captains. Players often forget to use the correct number of scooters, to repair their fence, and to tell an opponent to get off a scooter when a goal is scored or the rim has been hit. Although captains play the game like everyone else, they have some specific responsibilities.

The captains' responsibilities are as follows:

1. Watch for balls that are scored or hit the rim.
2. Remind teammates who make a goal or hit the rim to go repair a fence (walk over and place one ball on a cone) and retrieve a scooter from an opponent to place behind the repaired cone.
3. Stay aware of how many scooters the other team is allowed to use—otherwise, the opposing team will probably continue to use the scooters.

Rules and Safety

1. Players may not throw downed tennis balls.
2. Players must yell "Boo-Yah" when knocking a ball off a cone, scoring a goal, or hitting the rim.

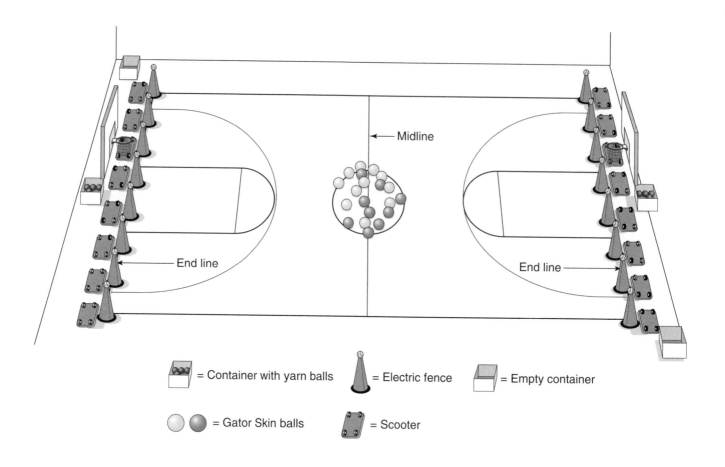

= Container with yarn balls   = Electric fence   = Empty container

= Gator Skin balls   = Scooter

3. Players who make a goal or hit the rim must yell "Boo-Yah" to notify everyone of their accomplishment before going back in time through a portal to repair part of their team's electric fence.

4. Players on scooters may only travel through the holes or damaged areas of the electric fence to go collect Boo-Yah and return to their team's container.

5. Only players on hovercrafts may cross the midline to retrieve Boo-Yah to bring back to their container, one Boo-Yah at a time. Players may not throw Boo-Yah and must take the Boo-Yah all the way to their team's bucket. When tired, players may switch and allow other teammates to use the hovercrafts.

6. Players are not allowed to guard or touch the electric fence except when traveling through time to repair one cone.

7. The number of balls knocked off the cones should equal the number of hovercrafts the teams are using. Some teams will forget to use hovercrafts because they are too focused on throwing the balls. The game may need to be paused to remind players that the main objective is to use all the hovercrafts to get as much Boo-Yah as possible.

8. If opponents are asked to give up their scooters and they have Boo-Yah, they must hand the scooter over and return the Boo-Yah to the opposing team before going back to their side. A player can prove that the hovercraft must be returned by pointing at the part of the fence that was repaired.

9. The team with all or the most Boo-Yah at the end of class or a round wins.

Variations

1. Instead of using the basketball goal, provide a different target at a lower level and a shorter distance.
2. Allow an unlimited number of defenders to guard the cones. Or designate 2, 3, or 4 defenders per team, using colored jerseys to distinguish each team's defenders.
3. Allow players to ride the scooters in various ways, such as the Bear and Alligator crawl or any way deemed safe by the teacher.
4. Eliminate the rule of hitting the rim to make it harder to go back in time.
5. Put two scooters behind each cone to allow more players the opportunity to use scooters. This works especially well with classes or 50 or more.

BOUNCE BRIGADE

Objective

This wacky game reinforces cooperation, eye–hand coordination, patience, strategy, and teamwork.

Equipment

Needs are based on a class of 48 students (8 teams of 6 players; teams should have at least 4 and no more than 8 players).

▶ 5-gallon buckets (8)

▶ Cans or plastic buckets, 90- to 110-ounce (2 per team; the school cafeteria is a great place to obtain cans and plastic buckets; if you use cans be sure there are no sharp edges)

▶ Hula hoops (1 per team)

▶ Ricochet balls, also known as Z-balls or reaction balls (1 per team; optional)

▶ Wiffle balls in different colors (24, 3 balls in the same color for each team; tennis balls may be substituted by marking 3 balls with the number 1, 3 balls with the number 2, and so on)

Procedure

Before students arrive, set out the eight buckets as depicted in the diagram. Place four hula hoops at each end of the gym and put three tennis balls, two cans, and one ricochet ball inside each hula hoop (see diagram for setup).

The object of the game is for teams to transfer each of their three balls and the ricochet ball (if provided) to the buckets located at the opposite end of the gym. Teams race against each other to determine who will accomplish this feat the fastest. No positions are assigned. Players are responsible for choosing what equipment to use and how they want to contribute to the game.

Divide the class into eight teams of six and send each team to a hula hoop to sit down and await further instructions. Explain that each team must decide who will be Throwers and who will be Canners.

Play begins with one player standing inside the team's hoop to advance a ball to a teammate down the court. Throwers may toss or throw the balls, but one bounce and no more must occur before a Canner may catch a ball. Throwers and Canners may switch positions with each other any time during the game. Players must follow a Thrower–Canner progression to advance a ball down the court. For example, starting from inside the hoop, each Thrower must toss the ball and each Canner must catch the ball with the can after allowing the ball to bounce one time. The same Thrower or a new Thrower will then advance toward the bucket to allow the Canner to toss the ball out of the can for the Thrower to catch it after allowing the ball to bounce one time (see illustration). Teams can split up and work as partners with multiple teams in the Thrower–Canner progression or work in groups of three or more to advance a ball toward a bucket. Any ball that is caught before bouncing once or is caught after bouncing more than one time must go back to the beginning to be reentered into the game.

Any ball that is dropped must also be returned to the beginning. Each team continues the Thrower–Canner progression until they score by bouncing a ball into the bucket. All misses result in returning the ball to the team's hoop and starting over. The only exception to this rule is with the ricochet ball: It is advanced the same way as the other balls, but it must be dropped (not bounced) into the bucket by a Canner.

Teams need to be encouraged to not give up because patience is often tested due to the degree of accuracy needed to get the balls into the buckets. Each team continues the process of advancing a ball to each of the buckets. The first team to get one ball into each bucket the fastest is the winner for that round. Clean up and start a new round.

▶ *Thrower–Canner progression.*

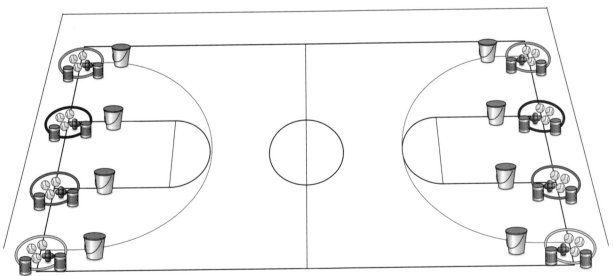

 = Bucket    = Cans   = Balls   = Hoop

Rules and Safety

1. A ball cannot leave a team's hoop unless a player stands in the hoop to throw it to another teammate.

2. Balls can only be advanced by one bounce. All balls that are dropped, caught before bouncing, or bounce more than once must go back to the beginning.

3. All Throwers or Canners who catch balls may rotate their body to bounce the balls to teammates. Players may not move toward a bucket while in possession of a ball.

4. Players can make overhand or underhand throws to teammates. Make sure players are careful with the ricochet balls since they are heavier than the other balls.

5. A player may be in possession of only one ball at a time.

6. Players must follow the Thrower–Canner progression to advance any ball down the court. Canners may not shield balls into the can with their bodies and may not touch a ball with their hands.

7. Teammates may use any grouping strategy to accomplish the task of getting balls into buckets. An assembly line works well, especially when a team gets to the last ball.

8. Each team must score in the buckets at the opposite end of the gym. A team may not have more than one ball in the same bucket.

Variation

Increase game duration by using additional balls or substituting other kinds of balls, especially balls with a unique bounce like the ricochet ball.

BOWL-A-HULA

Objective

This zany, action-packed game reinforces spatial awareness, hula-hoop manipulation, and bowling for accuracy. There are three excellent versions of Bowl-a-Hula. Try each one to determine which version your students enjoy the most.

Version 1 Equipment

Needs for each version are based on a class of 54.

- Gator Skin or playground balls, 8.5 inch (6)
- Hula hoops in any size (48)

Version 1 Procedure

Place six Gator Skin balls in the center of the gym and randomly spread the hoops around the gym. When students arrive, select six players to be Bowlers and six players to be Hula Helpers; all other students are Rollers. Instruct Bowlers to go to the center and sit down with one ball in their lap. Have each Hula Helper go and sit in one corner of the gym or against any wall. Instruct Rollers to sit down inside a hula hoop and await further instructions.

The object of this version is for the Bowlers to capture or stop as many Rollers as possible. On your signal, the Rollers begin rolling their hula hoop all over the gym, attempting to avoid Bowlers. Bowlers may stand still or run and attempt to roll the Gator Skin balls through the Rollers' hoops. (A demonstration of the correct way to bowl is recommended.) Rollers must stop and begin hula hooping or hula jumping if a Bowler rolls a ball through their hoop. Rollers must continue hula hooping or jumping until freed by a Hula Helper. The job of a Hula Helper is to move around the gym saving captured Rollers by taking the Roller's hoop, "reenergizing" the Roller using the hoop, and returning the hoop (see illustration). To reenergize the Roller, the Roller stands inside the hoop while the Hula Helper waves the hoop from head to toe and back up.

Once reenergized, Rollers are free to continue rolling the hoops around the gym. Stop the game after 5 to 10 minutes and instruct Bowlers and Hula Helpers to switch positions with Rollers. You may also choose to have Rollers switch roles with the Hula Helper immediately after being freed.

Version 1 Rules and Safety

1. Bowlers must bowl or roll balls.
2. Rollers must continually roll their hoop and may not pick it up to avoid a ball. Encourage Rollers to pay attention where they roll their hoop to look out for the safety of others. Players must pick up the hoop if it falls and then continue rolling.
3. Rollers can only be captured if the ball clearly goes through their hoop.

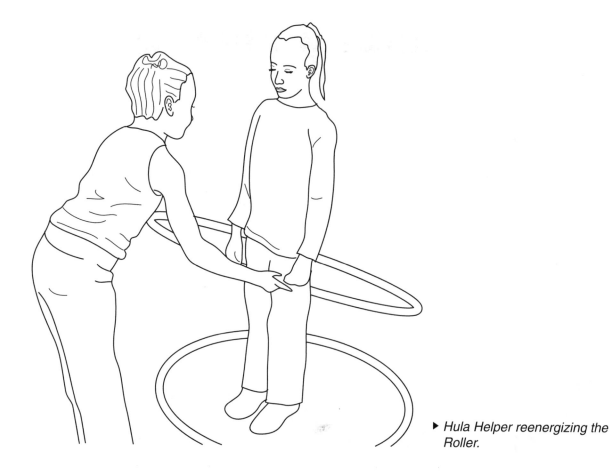

▶ *Hula Helper reenergizing the Roller.*

Version 1 Variation

Allow Hula Helpers to tap (reenergize) captured Rollers with a noodle if there are not enough hoops to go around.

Version 2 Equipment

Needs for each version are based on a class of 54.

- ▶ Gator Skin or playground balls (1 each in red, blue, green, purple, yellow, and orange)
- ▶ Hula hoops in any size (48, at least 8 each in red, blue, green, purple, yellow, and orange or marked with colored tape)
- ▶ Jerseys to designate teams (optional but recommended)

Version 2 Procedure

Version 2 setup, procedures, and rules are the same as in version 1 with the following exception: Each Bowler is assigned one of the six colored Gator Skin balls and each Hula Helper is assigned one of the six colored hoops. Now, for example, the red Bowler may only bowl the Gator Skin ball through players who are rolling red hoops and the red Hula Helper may only reenergize captured players with red hoops. The object of version 2 is for the Bowlers to capture as many Rollers from their color as possible.

Version 3 Equipment

Needs for each version are based on a class of 54.

▸ Gator Skin or playground balls (1 each in red, blue, green, purple, yellow, and orange)

▸ 36-inch hula hoops or same size hoops (48, at least 8 each in red, blue, green, purple, yellow, and orange; if different colored hoops aren't available, mark hoops with colored tape)

Version 3 Procedure

Place all six Gator Skin balls in the center of the gym and randomly spread the hoops around the gym. When students arrive, select six players to be Bowlers and have them go to the center and sit down with one colored ball in their lap. There are no Hula Helpers in version 3, so all other students are Rollers. Instruct Rollers to sit down inside a hula hoop and await further instructions. The object of version 3 is for Bowlers to capture as many Rollers as possible in order to build the most hula huts.

On your signal, the Rollers begin rolling their hula hoop anywhere within the gym boundaries without stopping, attempting to avoid the Bowler who has their color. For example, a Roller with a blue hoop tries to avoid the Bowler with the blue Gator Skin ball. Bowlers may stand still or run and attempt to roll their Gator Skin ball through the hoops in their color. Rollers must stop, go outside the basketball court boundaries or predetermined area, and begin hula hooping or hula jumping until five other Rollers from their color have also been captured. The six captured Rollers with the same hoop color work together to build a hula hut.

You should provide a quick, one-time demonstration of how to build a hula hut. Place one hoop on the ground (the foundation). Place two hoops on the inside edge of the foundation on opposite sides. Lean them together at 45-degree angles. Place two more

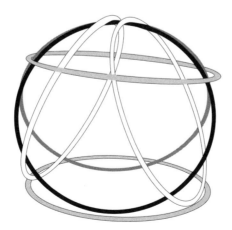

▸ *Hula hut.*

hoops on the inside edge of the foundation on opposite sides of the other two hoops. Lean them together at 45-degree angles over the first two hoops. Place the sixth hoop, which is the roof, on top to hold the walls in place (see illustration).

All six captured players may retrieve their hoops and reenter the game after successfully building their hula hut. Bowlers earn one point for every hut that is built of their color during the round, which lasts from 5 to 15 minutes. The Roller team with the fewest huts earns one point. Instruct Bowlers to switch with a Roller from their color, and start a new game.

Version 3 Rules and Safety

1. Bowlers must roll balls at the hoops of Rollers with the same color as the Bowler.

2. Rollers must continually roll their hoop and may not pick up hoops or lay them flat on the ground to avoid a ball. Encourage Rollers to pay attention where they roll their hoop to look out for the safety of others. Rollers must pick up and continue rolling the hoop if it falls.

3. Rollers must stop, go outside the boundaries, and hula hoop or hula jump every time they are captured until six Rollers from the same color have been captured, at which point they build a hula hut. Rollers may reenter the game upon completing this task.

BOWLING BLITZ

Objective

This game improves bowling for accuracy while placing students in nonstop defensive situations.

Equipment

Needs are based on a class of 60 students.

▷ Bowling pins (55)
▷ Gator Skin balls (50-100)
▷ Traffic cones, 28-inch (10-15, enough to designate a large oval around the small circle in the middle of the gym; the oval should be big enough to hold 55 or more players), or Border Patrol padded panels (found in most physical education catalogues)

Procedure

Before students arrive, place bowling pins on the gym floor. Next, use the traffic cones to create a large oval around the small circle in the middle of the gym. Finally, place 50 to 100 Gator Skin balls in the middle of the gym (see diagram for setup). When students arrive, select five players to be Blitzers and send them to the center of the gym. (The number of Blitzers can be increased for larger classes and decreased for smaller classes.) The rest of the players are Protectors. Have Protectors each get one bowling pin, place it on any sideline or end line, and stay next to the pin, awaiting further instructions. Encourage Protectors to spread out.

The object of the game is for the Protectors to keep their bowling pin from being destroyed by the Blitzers. Blitzers begin the game by rolling balls in attempt to knock down bowling pins. Blitzers must stay inside the circle of cones. When out of ammunition, Blitzers may go anywhere to collect balls, but they may not begin rolling balls until they are completely inside the circle of cones.

Bowling pins must always be placed on a sideline or end line and may not be touched once the game begins. Protectors must stand behind their pin with their back facing the wall. Protectors always play defense and must carefully guard their bowling pins by leaning over the pin and knocking balls away (see illustration). Protectors may not retrieve and roll balls. Protectors go to the center and become Blitzers when their pins are destroyed. Once a pin is down, it stays down, even if it was knocked down accidentally. The last five players with pins standing are the winners for the round. Reset the pins, return the balls to the center, and instruct the winners to go to the center to be the Blitzers in the next round.

▶ *Protectors guarding the pins.*

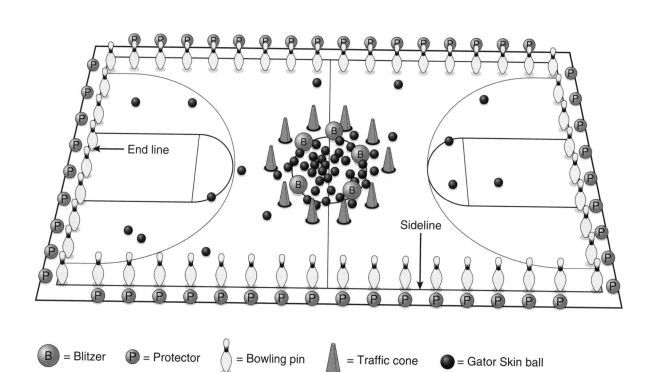

B = Blitzer   P = Protector   = Bowling pin   = Traffic cone   = Gator Skin ball

Rules and Safety

1. When out of ammunition, Blitzers may go anywhere to collect balls, but they may not begin rolling balls until they are completely inside the circle of cones.

2. Bowling pins must be placed on the sideline and may not be touched once the game begins.

3. Protectors must stand behind their pin with their back facing the wall.

4. Protectors may not retrieve and roll balls.

5. Protectors immediately go to the center and become Blitzers when their pins are destroyed.

6. Once a pin is down, it stays down, even if it was knocked down accidentally.

Strategy

Take a moment to discuss how Blitzers could use teamwork to focus all rolled balls at individual protectors. It is much harder to defend several balls at once as opposed to one ball every now and then.

BRYG IT ON

Objective

This is a high-energy game of fleeing and dodging where focus and teamwork are essential for success.

Equipment

Needs are based on a class of 48 students (4 teams of 12 players).

- ▶ Hula hoops (1 each in blue, red, yellow, and green)
- ▶ Sonic Flag-A-Tag or Velcro flag belts (12 belts each in blue, red, yellow, and green, with 2 flags per belt; juggling scarves placed at the hips can be substituted)

Procedure

Before classes arrive, place a hula hoop in each corner of the gym. Inside each hoop, place all 12 of the flag belts that are the same color as the hoop.

When students arrive, instruct them to put on a flag belt and sit down beside their color of hoop and await further instructions. Explain that the BRYG in BRYG It On represents Blue, Red, Yellow, and Green. Knowing the BRYG rule will help students remember that blue always chases red, red always chases yellow, yellow always chases green, and green always chases blue.

The object of the game is to be the team, or color, with the most flags still connected to their belts when the time limit expires. Each team begins running around the gym, attempting to pull the flags based on the BRYG rule (you may also choose another locomotor movement besides running). Remind students that they are not only trying to pull flags, they are also trying to avoid the team who is trying to pull their flags. After pulling a flag, players must immediately drop it to the ground. The game continues until both of a player's flags have been pulled. Players who lose both flags immediately stop and form a bridge by getting in the push-up position and then arching the midsection of the body toward the ceiling. All players must remain in this position until a teammate has completely crawled under their bridge (see illustration). Remind players that they must always look out for teammates who have formed bridges, because a team will be eliminated if all members lose their flags.

Once freed, players must find their flags, go and stand inside their team's hula hoop, and put the flags on before reentering the game. All players are safe while inside their team's hoop. Play continues until time expires (this can be either 10-20 minutes or when the class appears to be exhausted). Once the time has expired, teams quickly gather and count the flags that are still connected to their belts.

Performing a 10-second countdown during which players from the same team gather and count up attached flags helps keep the game moving. The team with the most flags wins that round. Start a new round after everyone has retrieved their flags from the ground, gone to their hoop, and reattached their flags.

▶ *A player forms a bridge to free a teammate.*

Rules and Safety

1. Players must follow the BRYG rule: Blue always chases red, red always chases yellow, yellow always chases green, and green always chases blue. Remind each team that the team they chase is not the team that chases them.

2. Bridges are formed only after both of a player's flags have been pulled.

3. A teammate must completely crawl under the bridge to free a player. Once free, players must stand inside their team's hoop while they reattach their flags. Only players who are reattaching flags can use the safe zone.

4. A team is out of the round if all its players are in a bridge.

5. Players must perform the locomotor movement determined by the teacher.

6. Players may not protect or hide flags; belts must clearly display flags.

7. Players may not reattach flags or count flags on the ground when the time limit has expired. Cheaters will disqualify their team.

Variations

1. Be creative with this game and come up with new methods for freeing players, or have players earn their flags back by performing a predetermined skill or exercise.

2. To keep teams even, allow the extra players to be Special Agents. Special Agents wear jerseys and are allowed to pull any team's flags.

3. Eliminate the BRYG rule for K through 1 students.

4. Disregard the BRYG rule or make up a new color-code rule if other flag colors must be substituted.

5. For smaller classes, use three flag colors. For example, blue always chases red, red always chases yellow, and yellow always chases blue (BRY).

BUILDING BLOCKS

Objective

This game requires teamwork and critical thinking in a race to build the tallest building. The idea of building blocks may also be used to introduce and reinforce the FITT principle of exercise (Frequency, Intensity, Time, and Type).

Equipment

Needs are based on a class of 60 students.

- Hula hoops (12)
- Noodle pieces, mini noodles, or foam building blocks (300-1000; create mini noodles by cutting long foam noodles into 1- or 2-inch pieces—an electric carving knife works best)
- Storage containers (2)
- Yardstick (1)

Procedure

Put noodle pieces in the large containers and place the containers at opposite ends of the gym against each end wall. Rest six hoops flat on the floor against the wall at each end of the gym (see diagram for setup). When classes arrive, instruct students to get into groups of five, choose a captain, go to one of the hoops, and sit down to await further instructions.

The object of the game is for each team to build the tallest building by earning as many building blocks (mini noodles) as they can. Each group must quickly brainstorm and determine how to travel from their hoop to the opposite end line and back in order to collect one building block. Teams must keep in mind the following rules:

1. All five players from each team must be connected or in contact with each other while traveling to the end line and back.

2. Teams must come up with a new way to travel to the end line and back each time they attempt to earn a building block. A team may not perform the same locomotor skill twice. For example, all five players might hold hands and skip to the end line and back, after which they may not travel by skipping again. The first four or five skills will be easy, but creating new ways to travel will gradually get tougher, requiring teammates to use critical thinking to come up with more ideas.

3. Teams earn one building block at a time with each new locomotor skill performed to the end line and back. Upon returning to their hoop, each captain goes to the container on their side of the gym, grabs one mini noodle, and drops it inside their hoop before the team performs a new movement.

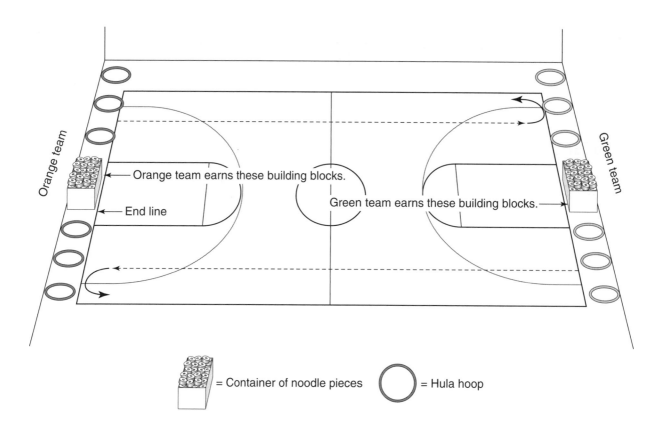

= Container of noodle pieces   = Hula hoop

Teams may begin constructing their building at any time by stacking building blocks (see illustration on page 27). Help teams realize that they must be careful when stacking the building blocks because most mini noodles differ in shape and width. Team members must work together when attempting to build the tallest and sturdiest building. Encourage teams not to spend too much time building because they may lose valuable time for collecting more building blocks. All teams must return to their hoops when the time limit designated by the teacher has expired or when there are no more building blocks. Be sure to provide a 1- to 3-minute countdown to allow each team the opportunity to finish building.

Use the yardstick to measure each team's building height to determine which team has the tallest building. After the countdown, buildings may not be repaired if they fall down. Clean up and start a new game once a team has been declared a winner.

Optional: Take this opportunity to discuss the "building blocks" of a healthy lifestyle: cardiovascular fitness, flexibility, nutrition, and physical strength and endurance. You can also apply the FITT principle (Frequency, Intensity, Time, and Type) to each building block. For example, explain that cardiovascular fitness is a crucial building block of health. Aerobic workouts burn calories, reduce stress, and decrease the risk of heart disease. You can apply the FITT principle to cardiovascular fitness by discussing how frequently students should exercise (3 to 5 times a week), the intensity of the exercise (how hard the exercise makes your heart beat), the length of time they should exercise (20 to 60 minutes), and the type of exercise they should do (something they enjoy doing).

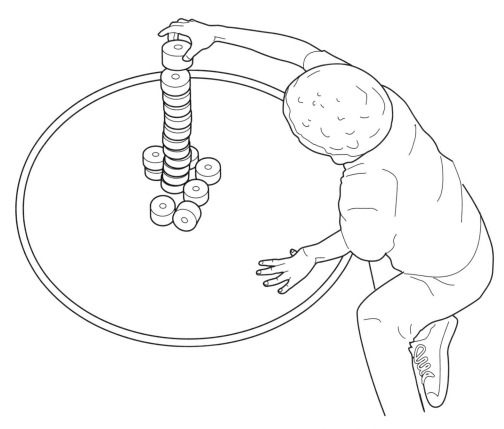

▶ *Constructing the building using building blocks (mini noodles).*

Rules and Safety

1. All players in a group must participate and be in contact with one another to earn a building block. Teams must go down to the end line and back before retrieving a building block. No running is allowed at any time!

2. Teams must find new ways to travel to an end line and back in order to earn a building block. Also, teams must avoid crashing into other teams.

3. Teams may collect only one building block at a time.

4. Teams may begin constructing their building at any time by stacking the building blocks. Teammates may not stay behind to build while the rest of the team earns blocks. Buildings' design and structure may vary.

5. All teams must return to their hoop when the designated time limit has expired or when there are no more building blocks. The teacher then performs a 1- to 3-minute countdown. Teams must complete the building process during the countdown.

6. The teacher travels from hoop to hoop measuring each team's building to determine which is the tallest.

When given the opportunity to develop new ways to travel, students may come up with some potentially unsafe ideas, such as carrying teammates in various ways. If the class is mature enough, let teams explore the endless traveling ways they can use. You will be amazed at many of the fascinating ideas that teams come up with. If you are in doubt about your students' ability to make safe choices, then you must determine which of the following rules to implement:

1. Players, if you think an idea is potentially dangerous, do not do it!
2. No carrying teammates on each other's shoulders.
3. Teams must walk when carrying a teammate.

Variations

1. Increase or decrease the size of each group based on class size.
2. Create a different method for earning building blocks.
3. Allow teams to collect more than one block at a time. This will greatly increase the size and structure of the buildings.

C.H.A.O.S.

Objective

This is an invigorating fitness game where teamwork and strategy can easily be confused with "C.H.A.O.S."

Equipment

Needs are based on a class of 48 students (16 teams of 3 students).

- ▸ Hula hoops (15)
- ▸ Jerseys (15)
- ▸ Noodles, whole or cut in half (3)
- ▸ Scooters (15)
- ▸ 4 each, preferably in the same color, of 15 different items (60 total items, such as balloons, beanbags, birdees, bowling pins, checkers, flags, Gator Skin balls, lummi sticks, noodle pieces, poly spots, pucks, scarves, tennis balls, Wiffle balls, yarn balls)

Procedure

Place 15 hula hoops randomly around the gym. Put one scooter, one jersey, and four of the same item inside each hoop. Place three noodles in the center of the gym (see diagram for setup).

The object of the game is for each team to keep their four items while stealing items from the other teams. As students arrive, instruct them to form teams of three, choose one hula hoop to sit beside, sit down, and await further instructions. The team of three without a hula hoop will go to the center of the gym and will be called the noodle players. Explain that players from each team, except for the noodle players, must choose one of three roles: scooter, jersey, or running. Scooter players sit on their scooter and travel around the gym stealing items from other teams' hula hoops. Jersey players wear the jersey and run around the gym stealing back their original four items. Running players run around the gym stealing other teams' items but not stealing back any of their team's original four items. Players may steal only one item at a time, taking it to their team's hoop before they steal another item.

The job of the three noodle players is to use their noodle to tag players carrying stolen items. Once tagged, the player must drop the item, allowing the noodle player to pick it up and return it to the center circle of the gym. Any player may earn back one of their team's items that a noodle player put into the center circle by performing 10 jumping jacks or whatever exercise you determine before each round.

Explain that after each round, the acronym of C.H.A.O.S. will be used to describe each team's award level. Each team earns a level based on how many of their original four items are inside their team's hoop. If teams have none of their original items but have

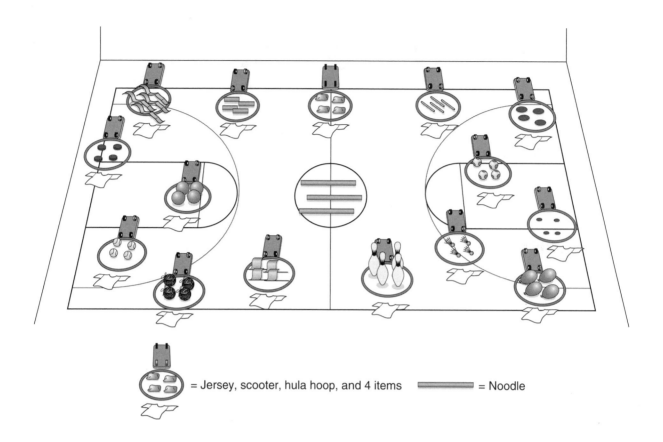

 = Jersey, scooter, hula hoop, and 4 items   = Noodle

at least one item from another team, they earn level C, which means that the team is Cool. One remaining original item earns level H, which means that the team is Hot. Two remaining original items earns level A, which means that the team is Awesome. Three remaining original items earns level O, which means that the team is Out of Sight. Four remaining original items earns level S, which means that the team is Super Human.

To begin the game, players must work together, choosing one of the three roles to perform for that round. Then each team member begins traveling around the gym performing their specific duties. The ultimate goal is to be the only team to earn level S. After 10 minutes or whatever amount of time you deem necessary, stop the game and determine what level each team has earned (C, H, A, O, or S). The only award the noodle players may earn is the title of Super Human if no teams were able to earn Super Human status. After you determine each team's level, teams retrieve their original four items. Perform a 10-second countdown to allow players to retrieve the items, and perform another 10-second countdown to allow each team to switch roles before starting the next round. Also, after each round, allow noodle players to switch with someone new from one of the 15 teams to give others the opportunity to be noodle players.

Rules and Safety

1. Each team except for the noodle team must have a player performing one of the three roles. Players must follow the exact rules governing their role. There is no role switching during a round.

2. Scooter players must be seated while riding the scooter.

3. Players may only take one item at a time and must return it to their team's hoop before stealing another item. Players may not hand off an item to another teammate.

4. Any player who is tagged must drop the stolen item before going to steal another item.

5. Noodle players may tag anyone to take away a stolen item, but they must pick up the dropped item and return it to the center circle before tagging anyone else. Noodle players may not steal items directly from hula hoops.

6. Any player can go to the center to earn back one of their original four items by performing 10 repetitions of the required exercise. Noodle players may not tag and take back the item from players who have just completed an exercise.

7. Play Rock, Paper, Scissors to settle any arguments over whether someone was tagged before placing an item in their hoop.

8. No defense! Teams may not guard their hoops.

9. The noodle players will be declared Super Human if no teams earned that level.

Variations

1. If the number of students is not divisible by three, have the extra players be noodle players for one round and then switch them with other players before beginning the next round.

2. Eliminate the noodle players if the game is too complex for students in grades K through 1. Each team simply steals from each other. Don't worry about the levels; just promote being active. Allow two scooter players per group.

3. Do not allow teams to earn back items stolen by noodle players.

4. There are lots of possible variations, so you decide what twist you want to add. Your students will have to listen carefully to these instructions and think of their own strategies to win this challenging game!

CROCODILE MILE

Objective

This game implements teamwork and strategy in a fast-paced situation where quickness and agility are necessary to avoid the ferocious crocodiles.

Equipment

Needs are based on a class of 60 students (20 teams of 3 students).

- 5-gallon buckets (2; 1 per team for storing each team's flies to avoid confusion of whose flies are whose)
- Hula hoops (36)
- Poly spots (18)
- Scooters in two different colors (3 of each color, such as red and purple)
- Traffic cones, 28-inch (15-20)
- Yarn balls or noodle pieces in the same colors as the scooters (50-100 of each color; substitute two other colors if these colors are unavailable). It is recommended to place each set of 50-100 yarn balls into a container for easy transport to each end wall.

Scenario

Deep in the heart of the African jungle flows the dangerous Crocodile Mile River. This river is most dangerous because of its infestation of giant crocodiles. The entire frog species must avoid extinction by gathering enough food to survive. Each frog family must work together using their available lily pads to safely navigate the Crocodile Mile, avoiding the ferocious crocodiles. Remember, these crocodiles are very hungry, so beware!

Procedure

Before students arrive, place nine sets (2 hula hoops and 1 poly spot equals 1 set) at each end of the gym. Place three red and three purple scooters in the center of the gym. Next, place a container of yarn balls at each end wall of the gym. Finally, place a bucket at each end of the midline. Place traffic cones on both sides of the gym approximately 6 feet apart, using the free-throw line as a reference (see diagram for setup). Select six students to be crocodiles and instruct them to sit in the center of the gym with a scooter in their lap. Instruct all other students to get into groups, or families, of three and go sit at one stack of lily pads, which consists of two hula hoops and one poly spot. One student is the frog and two are the dragonflies; have students decide which role they want to play. If there are one or two extra students, create one or two groups of four, adding an extra hoop to their stack. Players on one side of the gym are bullfrogs and players on the other side are tree frogs. Read the scenario to the class.

The object of the game is for all frog families to travel through the marsh and river (across the gym to the opposite side) on their three lily pads, avoiding all crocodiles as they gather flies (yarn balls) and then storing the flies in the container at their home area.

Each team consists of one frog and two dragonflies. Frogs must always be on a lily pad to travel through the marsh and river (see illustration). The dragonflies work together by picking up and moving lily pads, implementing the best strategy to allow their frog to quickly advance toward the flies. All crocodiles are inside the river boundaries designated by the traffic cones and may only attack a frog team who is carrying a fly within the river boundaries. A crocodile attacks a team by tagging the frog and taking the fly to a crocodile bucket. Crocodiles may not attack again until they have dropped the fly into one of their buckets. Crocodiles may attack frogs inside a hula hoop within river boundaries, but they may not attack frogs that are standing on a poly spot. The poly spot is each team's safe lily pad.

Crocodiles on red scooters may only attack tree frogs and crocodiles on purple scooters may only attack bullfrogs. Crocodiles know whom to attack by the color of fly a team is carrying. For example, crocodiles on red scooters may only attack frog teams who are attempting to cross the river to drop off a red fly at their home area. Frog teams are safe from harm once they are in either marsh area or the frog is on the poly spot. Frog teams must transport their fly all the way back to their home area and drop it off into their team's bucket before switching frogs to go get another fly. The frog team with the most flies is the winner for that round. Clean up and start a new round.

▶ *The frog (standing on the poly spot) works with the dragonflies (players with hoops) to avoid the crocodile (player on scooter) and cross the river.*

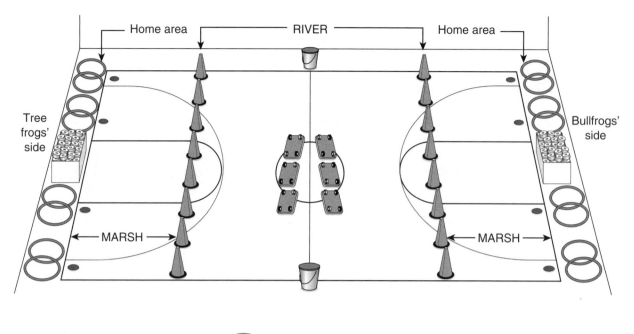

Rules and Safety

1. Frogs may only advance by jumping from lily pad to lily pad. A frog is considered on a lily pad while standing on the poly spot or inside the hula hoop. Frogs may not move or slide the lily pad.

2. A team may immediately turn around and go back, jumping from lily pad to lily pad, to get another fly if a crocodile takes their fly.

3. Crocodiles may not attack frogs on poly spots or frogs in the marsh.

4. Frogs may not hide flies as they move through the river. Dragonflies may not have possession of a fly.

5. Frogs may only take one fly at a time. A dropped fly must be left for the crocodiles. Flies are not to be thrown at any time.

6. Crocodiles must place a captured fly in their bucket before attacking another frog.

7. Frogs may move forward or backward on lily pads at any time.

8. Only dragonflies are allowed to pick up and move lily pads.

Variations

1. Decrease the number of crocodiles to make the game easier and shorter or vice versa.

2. Eliminate the use of crocodiles with students in grades K through 1.

3. Increase difficulty by eliminating the safety poly spot and replacing it with a hula hoop.

4. Place one trash can at each end of the gym for each side to place their flies. At the end of a round, count which side has the most flies in the can. That team (bullfrogs or tree frogs) is declared the winner of the round.

EMPIRE MANIA

Objective

This teamwork game is excellent for large or small classes, indoors or outdoors! It guarantees participation and an aerobic workout while emphasizing adaptability, problem solving, and spontaneity. There are two excellent versions of Empire Mania. Try both to determine which version your students enjoy the most.

Version 1 Equipment

Needs are based on a class of 20 to 80 students.

▸ Gator Skin balls (1-4; having more than 1 ball increases the difficulty but shortens the duration of the game)

Version 1 Procedure

Instruct students to find a personal space somewhere in the gym. Determine which student gets to be the first Maniac (it is easiest to pick the person with the closest birthday).

On your signal, the Maniac runs and attempts to roll or throw the Gator Skin ball until the ball contacts a player who is running around trying to avoid being captured. (Note that Gator Skin or foam balls are essential for preventing pain.) Once the ball contacts someone, that person has been captured and must join the Maniac's empire.

The object of this version is for the Maniac and his captured teammates to capture everyone on the loose. The last player captured by the Maniac's team gets to be the Maniac for the next round.

Version 1 Rules and Safety

1. The Maniac and captured players cannot move while in possession of a ball, with one exception: The Maniac is allowed to move around the gym until she captures her first player on the loose.

2. All captured players in possession of a ball must pass the ball to other teammates or throw or roll the ball to capture players on the loose.

3. All captured players who do not have a ball may move anywhere around the gym. A captured player may follow any noncaptured player in order to catch or field a ball and then hit that player.

4. Players must immediately join the empire once a ball contacts them at the shoulders or below.

5. There are no boundaries. Players may move anywhere within the gym. If playing outside, use traffic cones or chalk lines to designate the playing area.

Encourage the Maniac and captured players to use teamwork. For example, they might get the ball as close as possible to players on the loose by making multiple passes to run down or tire out even the most elusive and cunning players.

Version 2 Equipment

Needs are based on a class of 20 to 80 students.

▸ Gator Skin balls (1 each in red, blue, green, and orange)
▸ Jerseys (5-20 each in red, blue, green, and orange, separated by color and piled in each of the four corners of the gym)

Version 2 Procedure

Version 2 is similar to version 1, but with exciting new twists!

Place a Gator Skin ball and jerseys in the same color in each of the four corners. Choose four students to be Maniacs and send them to a corner to get the Gator Skin ball and a jersey in their color. Instruct all other students to find a space somewhere in the gym.

On your signal, all Maniacs run and roll or throw the Gator Skin ball until the ball contacts a player on the loose (see illustration). Once the ball contacts someone, that person has been captured and must immediately join that Maniac's empire by putting on a jersey in the same color as the Maniac who captured them (remember, jerseys representing each color are at one of the four corners of the gym).

The object of version 2 is for the Maniacs and captured teammates to capture the most players. The last four free players are the starting four Maniacs in the next round, or you may select the Maniacs at your discretion.

▸ *A maniac trying to capture another player.*

Version 2 Rules and Safety

1. Maniacs and captured players cannot move while in possession of a ball. Players caught traveling with a ball cause a 10-second freeze for everyone on their team, as signaled by the teacher. There is one exception: The four Maniacs are allowed to move around the gym with a ball until they capture their first player. Also, encourage players not to hold the ball more than 5 seconds.

2. Players must immediately join the team that captured them.

3. Captured players cannot attempt to capture other players until they have gone to one of the four corners of the gym and put on the color of jersey based on the color of ball they were captured by.

4. Continue play until most if not all of the players are wearing a jersey.

5. All Maniacs and captured players can only pick up balls in their empire's color, which they then pass to a teammate or throw or roll to capture players on the loose. No throwing the balls at other players who are already part of an empire! If the ball is not the same color as the players' team, they must leave it on the ground.

6. Captured players who do not have a ball may move anywhere around the gym. A captured player may follow any noncaptured player in order to catch or field a ball and then throw it at that player.

7. There are no boundaries. Players may move anywhere within the gym. If playing outdoors, mark the playing area using traffic cones or chalk lines.

8. At the end of each round, instruct captured players to huddle around their Maniac while you perform a 10-second countdown. For example, all players hit by a red ball huddle around the red Maniac who started the game. The team with the most captured players is declared the winner of that round. You can also keep track of each empire's tally for each round and determine a class champion based on which team captured the most players overall.

Variations

1. Eliminate one or two colors if the class size is too small for four empires. This will lengthen the duration of each round.

2. Increase the difficulty and duration of the game by placing everyone on scooters.

3. Add one to two balls to each team, especially with extremely large classes.

FINESSE

Objective

Can you picture Gary Payton maneuvering through the defense for a sweet finger roll, Mia Hamm heading the soccer ball gracefully into the goal, or Tiger Woods effortlessly draining a 40-foot putt? These are examples of finesse.

In this game students develop and refine bowling, throwing, and Frisbee skills, learning to execute delicate movements with finesse.

Equipment

Needs are based on a class of 20 to 80 students.

- Foam or indoor Frisbees (50-75)
- Gator Skin balls (50-75)
- Jerseys (2 green, 2 orange)
- Hula hoops (10)
- Noodles in two different colors, such as green and orange (20 green, 20 orange)
- Poly spots (10)
- Scooters
- Trash cans (2)

Procedure

Before students arrive, place five hula hoops flat on the ground at each end wall and place one set of five poly spots in two different corners of the gym. Place all Frisbees and Gator Skin balls in the center circle. Next, place one trash can in the middle of each free throw line. Finally, place each team's noodles against the wall on their side (see diagram for setup).

The object of the game is to be the first team to successfully complete all three finesse levels. Explain that today's game involves finesse. Skilled athletes like Gary Payton, Mia Hamm, and Tiger Woods execute finesse with great skill and style. They are able to put that delicate "touch" on the ball that makes scoring look easy. The game of Finesse will help you focus on accuracy and mastering your skills of bowling and throwing at targets, while helping you realize that throwing hard is not always a wise choice.

Divide the class into two teams and send teams to opposite ends of the gym. Select one or two captains from each team. Instruct them to stand in the corner opposite their team's side and hold the five poly spots for level one (poly spots will only be used in level one).

To achieve level 1, each team must, without physically crossing the midline, throw or bowl balls in an attempt to get three balls inside each of the five hoops at the opposite end of the gym. When three balls are inside a hoop, a captain may remove the balls and place a poly spot inside the hoop to indicate that there is no need to get any more balls inside that hoop. A team may only advance to level 2 once each of the five hoops has a poly spot inside of them. Team captains help by rolling balls back to their teammates and placing poly spots inside their team's hoops.

Upon achieving level 1, captains run to their team's side yelling "Level 2!" In level 2, the teams throw Frisbees until one Frisbee lands completely inside each of the five hoops. One Frisbee inside a hoop indicates that there is no need to get any more Frisbees inside that hoop. It is possible that the opposing team will still be at level 1. If the other team is still at level 1, the captains of the team at level 2 must cross over the midline to retrieve Frisbees for their teammates since no other players may cross the midline and the other team is still throwing balls instead of Frisbees.

After completing level 2, the team begins level 3 by retrieving the noodles from the side wall and throwing them in any way necessary to get three noodles inside the trash can at the free throw line. If the opposing team is still at level 1 or 2, the captains must cross over the midline and retrieve noodles for their teammates. The first team to complete level 3 is declared the winner for that round. Clean up and start a new round.

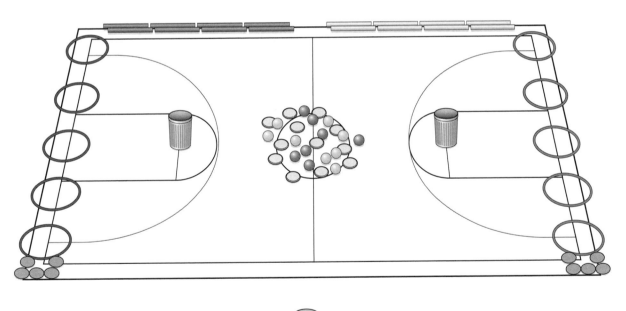

Rules and Safety

1. Players are not allowed to play defense or be near the opposing team's hula hoops. All players must clearly be attempting to achieve the next level. Also, balls or Frisbees must have completely stopped before being retrieved.
2. You may place a spot or Frisbee inside a hoop for a team if the opposing team violates a rule.
3. A team may not go to the next level until completing the previous level. Encourage each team to never give up, no matter how far ahead the opposing team is.
4. Each team's captains may cross the midline to gather Frisbees or noodles to help keep their team supplied. No other players may cross the midline to roll or throw a ball, Frisbee, or noodle.
5. Balls may not be removed from a hoop unless the requirement for that hoop has been met.
6. A player can handle only one ball, Frisbee, or noodle at a time.
7. A Frisbee that lands on a hoop does not count and should be removed. Also, Frisbees can be removed if there is more than one Frisbee inside a hoop. Remember, it only takes one Frisbee inside a hoop to meet that hoop's requirement.
8. Captains may switch with their teammates at any time during the game.

Variations

1. Select more captains when classes are very large.
2. Increase or decrease the difficulty by varying the distance of hoops from the wall or trash cans from the midline.
3. Make the requirements for accomplishing each level more or less difficult by increasing or decreasing the number of balls, Frisbees, or noodles needed to move on to the next level.
4. Remove level 3 for students in grades K through 2.

FLAG 'EM DOWN

Objective

This intense cardiovascular game encourages teamwork and is a great way to use flag belts.

Equipment

Needs are based on a class of 48 students (4 teams of 12 players).

▸ 5-gallon buckets (4)
▸ Hula hoops (2 each in blue, red, yellow, and green)
▸ Sonic Flag-A-Tag or Velcro flag belts (12 each in blue, red, yellow, and green, with two flags per belt), or Rip Flag belts, which have three flags permanently attached, or juggling scarves placed at the hips

Procedure

Before students arrive, distribute flag belts around the gym. Place one set of four hoops (blue, red, yellow, and green) against one end wall. At the opposite end wall, place a hoop with a bucket inside it directly across from its like-color hoop. Finally, place all 24 flags inside like-color hula hoops (see diagram for setup).

The object of the game is to be the team with the most flags still connected to their belts when the time limit expires. When classes arrive, instruct students to put on a flag belt, sit down beside their like-color hula hoop containing flags, and await further instructions.

In phase 1, each team must first transfer all of their flags from their hula hoop to their bucket at the opposite end of the gym. Each player may only be in possession of one flag at a time. Flags must be transferred from one teammate to another using an assembly line: Teammates link their feet (separating their legs and touching their foot against their neighbor's foot) and pass the flag down the line. A flag must be entered into the game and exited into a bucket by a player with one foot inside the hula hoop (see illustration). A flag cannot be passed to another teammate unless the players' feet are touching. The assembly line will probably not reach the hula hoop at the opposite end of the gym, so once a player passes a flag, that player goes down to the far end of the line. Teams must figure out the best possible strategies for quickly moving all of the flags to their bucket. Individual teams may split into groups of 2, 3, 4, or more to pass flags.

Phase 2 begins for a team when they get all their flags in their bucket. Players grab two flags out of their bucket and attach them to their flag belt. When all flags are attached, players begin pulling flags, one flag at a time, from any of the other teams who have made it to phase 2. The first team to complete phase 1 may have to wait a few minutes for another team to complete phase 1. If this occurs, encourage them to create strategies for pulling the other teams' flags.

▶ *Teammates link their feet and form an assembly line to pass a flag.*

Remind players to stay within designated boundaries. You may need to establish a consequence if players are violating rules. Any player pulling a flag must return the flag to its like-color hula hoop before going to pull another flag. Players who have at least one flag on their belt may continue pulling flags. Players who have lost both flags may retrieve and reattach flags from their team's bucket. Players who have lost both flags and do not have flags in their team's bucket must regain one or both flags by repeating the assembly line as implemented in phase 1, starting from their team's hula hoop. Players must team up with another player or players who have also lost both flags to form an assembly line to transfer flags to their bucket. Occasionally, some players will work together to replace a couple of flags in the bucket and then immediately attach them to their belt and leave the assembly line, not staying to help their teammates get flags. If this occurs, stop the game and take the opportunity to discuss character traits such as caring and fairness and how these traits can be demonstrated during the game.

Play continues until 10-20 minutes expire or when the class appears to be exhausted. Once the time has expired, do a quick count of flags that are still connected. The team with the most flags connected wins that round. Start a new round after all flags are inside the correct hula hoops.

Rules and Safety

1. Flags may not be advanced down an assembly line unless the teammates' feet are connected. (Hint: A team will cover more ground if they use wider stances.)
2. In phase 1, each player may be in possession of only one flag at a time.

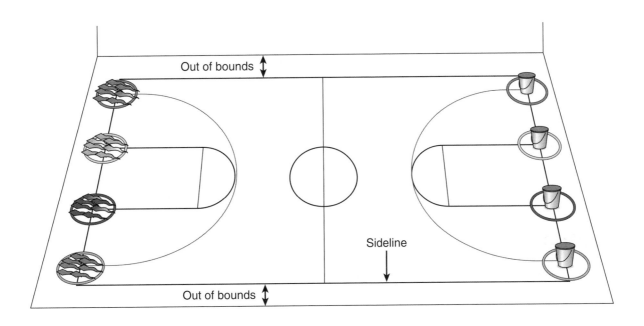

 = Flags in like-color hoop    = Like-color hoop with bucket

3. Throwing flags is not allowed.

4. Phase 2 begins for any team who has all of their flags in their bucket.

5. Players may not protect or hide flags. Belts must clearly display flags.

6. Players may pull only one flag at a time and must return the flag to the correct hula hoop before going to pull another flag.

7. Flags may not be stolen from a bucket.

8. Starting from their team's hoop, players must team up with partners who have also lost both flags to perform the assembly line to get their flags back to their team's bucket. Players with flags may assist their teammates in the assembly line but can have their flags stolen in the process.

9. Players may not reenter the game until one or both flags are on their belts.

10. The team with the most flags connected wins the round.

Variations

1. Eliminate a flag color if class size is small.

2. Add more flags to the game than there are players so that each team has extra flags in their bucket, thus reducing the number of assembly lines.

3. To keep teams even, allow the extra players to be Special Agents. Special Agents wear jerseys and are allowed to pull any team's flags.

4. If using Rip Flag belts (flags are sewn onto the actual belt), have players transfer the entire system from one side of the gym to the other during phase 1.

THE GREAT ESCAPE

Objective

This mind-boggling game improves problem solving, teamwork, strategy, and accuracy as each level challenges teams to make "the great escape."

Equipment

Needs are based on a class with at least 20 but no more than 80 students.

- ▶ Basketball goals at opposite sides of gym, set 8 feet high (2)
- ▶ Bowling pins (20-40; the more pins, the longer the game)
- ▶ Containers for bowling pins (2)
- ▶ Gator Skin balls or volleyball trainers (50-100)
- ▶ Jerseys to designate both teams (optional)
- ▶ Scooters (5-10; enough for a third of the class)
- ▶ Traffic cones and tennis balls (20 of each; 28-inch traffic cones work best because they are more stable and make knocking the tennis balls much harder in level 2). Wiffle or hockey balls may be substituted if tennis balls are unavailable.
- ▶ Wiffle, tennis, or hockey balls

Scenario

The evil king Darth Oman has imprisoned the entire town beneath his castle in his dark and dreadful dungeon. It is up to the townspeople to rely on each other and implement teamwork and problem-solving strategies to move through the many different levels of the dungeon to make "the great escape."

Procedure

Before students arrive, place 20 bowling pins on each end line and place one trash can at each side of the gym. Place 10 cones directly behind the bowling pins and put a tennis ball on top of each cone. The cones should be located against the end walls. Place the scooters against the sidewalls, and place the Gator Skin balls in the middle of the gym (see diagram for setup). Read the scenario to the class.

The object of the game is for each team to successfully accomplish three challenging levels in order to make "the great escape." Teams race against each other to complete all three levels the fastest. Level 1 involves breaking through the boneyard to destroy level 2's gunpowder explosives and get the keys to use in level 3 to lower the drawbridge and escape Darth Oman.

Divide the class into two teams, select one to three Gatekeepers for each team, and send each team to opposite ends of the gym to sit down and await further instructions. The Gatekeepers go to the end of the gym opposite their team.

In level 1, each team bowls balls from their half of the gym, attempting to completely destroy the boneyard (bowling pins) on the opposite end of the gym. Players may only retrieve and roll balls that are on their half of the gym. The Gatekeeper(s) retrieves each knocked over pin and places it in the barrel, helping to clear the way for the next task. Gatekeepers also assist their team by rolling balls to their team's side.

Once all of the pins are knocked over and the Gatekeeper(s) has placed all pins in the barrel, level 2 begins. In level 2, players get on the available scooters to cross over the midline of the gym and gather more ammunition (balls) for their team. While Musketeers (players on scooters) retrieve ammunition, players not on a scooter roll or throw balls to disarm the explosives by knocking the tennis balls off the traffic cones. Although some explosives may have been disarmed while rolling balls in level 1, players roll or throw balls to disarm all remaining explosives. (Hint: Throw the balls up high and off the walls to knock the tennis balls off.)

Level 3 begins when all explosives have been disarmed via knocking the tennis balls off the traffic cones. In this final level, players throw the Gator Skin balls (designated now as keys to the drawbridge) at the goal on the opposite end of the gym, attempting to make one goal. A ball that scores in the goal is the key that unlocks the drawbridge. The townspeople celebrate their victory by running across the midline to the opposite end of the gym to make the great escape.

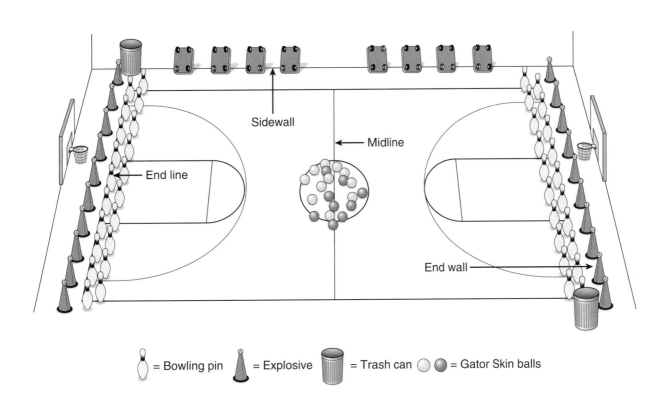

= Bowling pin   = Explosive   = Trash can   = Gator Skin balls

Rules and Safety

1. Players must roll balls during level 1. All players except for Musketeers may collect and roll balls from their side of the gym in all three phases.
2. Once level 1 is completed, all Gatekeepers return to their team's side.
3. Players may either roll or throw balls during levels 2 and 3.
4. Downed tennis balls may not be thrown!
5. Only players on scooters may cross the midline to retrieve balls during levels 2 and 3. Balls can be carried, thrown, or rolled back to each team's side. When tired, Musketeers may switch with other teammates. Using the scooters is not mandatory, although it is highly encouraged because it keeps teams supplied with balls.
6. No one is allowed to touch bowling pins or cones. Only Gatekeepers are allowed to remove downed pins.
7. Players are not allowed to guard the pins or cones in any way. All players must clearly be attempting to reach the next level.
8. The teacher may knock over pins or balls off cones for rule violations.
9. A team may not go to the next level until they have completed the previous level. Encourage each team to never give up, no matter how far ahead the opposing team may be.
10. Only one Gator Skin ball has to go through the hoop at the opposite end of the gym for a team to accomplish level 3 and win the game. All players run across the midline when their team has successfully accomplished level 3.

Variations

1. Increase the duration of the game by adding more bowling pins in level 1 or more cones with tennis balls in level 2.
2. Allow an unlimited number of defenders to guard the pins and explosives. Or, designate 2, 3, or 4 defenders per team (different colored jerseys will be necessary to distinguish defenders for different teams).
3. Have players skip, gallop, or perform other locomotor skills besides running.
4. Eliminate level 3 for grades K through 2, or, instead of using the basketball goal, provide a different target at a lower level and shorter distance.

H₂O NO!

Objective

In this game, students collaborate and use teamwork and quick decision making to save the nation from a deadly drought.

Equipment

Needs are based on a class of 48 students.

- ▸ 5-gallon buckets (8)
- ▸ Frisbees (4-6)
- ▸ Gator Skin balls, 6-inch (15-20 per team; smaller or larger balls may be used if necessary)
- ▸ Hockey sticks (20-28)
- ▸ Hula hoops (2)
- ▸ Jerseys to designate teams (optional)
- ▸ Noodles, green and orange (20-30 in each color; other colors may be substituted)
- ▸ Storage containers or barrels (2; hula hoops may be substituted)

Scenario

It is the year 2203 and every nation on earth has experienced a yearlong drought. The drought has led to a Red Alert Emergency because there is only enough water to survive a few more days. After months of searching, the world's top engineers have located an endless supply of pure water in an underground river. The engineers have very little time to transport and connect the pipeline and deliver the precious water to all the cities before everyone goes thirsty.

Procedure

Before students arrive, place 20 same-color noodles in a pile at each end wall and place two containers at opposite corners of the gym. Place two Frisbees beside each trash can and place two hula hoops at the other corners of the gym, opposite each other. Then place 15 Gator Skin balls inside each hula hoop and 10 hockey sticks beside each hula hoop. Finally, place four buckets on each side of the gym, against a side wall (see diagram for setup).

The object of the game is to successfully complete two challenging levels in order to save the world. Teams race against each other to determine who can complete both tasks the fastest. No positions are assigned; players are responsible for choosing how they want to contribute to the game. Level 1 involves transporting the pipeline to the underground river. Level 2 involves careful precision in connecting the pipeline to deliver the precious water to every city.

Divide the class into two teams and send teams to opposite ends of the gym to sit down and await further instructions. Read the scenario to the class.

In level 1, each team begins transporting their team's pipeline (noodles) from their end wall to the opposite end wall by tossing each pipeline to a teammate. All noodles that contact the ground are contaminated and must remain there until the Bucket Patrol picks them up and returns them to the original pile. The Bucket Patrol consists of any two to four players who want to carry a bucket. (Hint: The Bucket Patrol will work more efficiently if they use teamwork by scooping each end of a contaminated noodle into their buckets before returning it to the pile.)

Level 2 begins once all of a team's noodles are against the wall at the opposite end of the gym. In level 2, players lay pairs of pipeline on the floor and connect them to other pairs of pipeline (see illustration). As connections are made, other players begin transferring the water (Gator Skin balls) by grasping the balls using two hockey sticks like tongs and carefully placing the balls on top of the pipeline. Once the balls are on the pipeline, players begin advancing balls by pushing them down the pipeline toward the opposite end line. (Hint: Reshaping or straightening crooked pipeline makes it easier to transport balls.) Players pushing balls may only be in possession of one stick. Balls may not be touched or moved by hand. All balls that fall off the pipeline are contaminated and must remain on the floor until the Bucket Patrol or teammates with hockey sticks pick them up and return them to the hula hoop. Each ball that is successfully transported down the pipeline must be scooped into the water shovel (Frisbee) before being dropped into the water barrel.

Encourage the use of different teamwork strategies such as spreading teammates out and using multiple pipelines instead of one long pipeline. One long pipeline works well but is slow. Multiple teams with four sections of noodles can work very quickly to accomplish the same goal. The team to complete both levels the fastest is declared the winner for that round. Clean up and start a new round.

▶ *Players move the ball down the connected pipeline.*

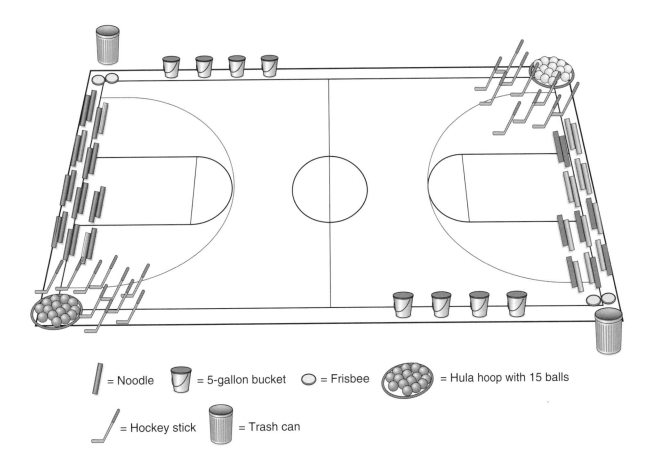

| = Noodle | = 5-gallon bucket | = Frisbee | = Hula hoop with 15 balls |

| = Hockey stick | = Trash can |

Rules and Safety

1. In level 1, all players must throw the pipeline from behind their end line, thus entering each pipeline into the playing area.

2. In level 1, a player in possession of a noodle cannot move forward or backward—they must throw or toss the noodle to a teammate. Players in possession of a noodle may only turn clockwise or counterclockwise without advancing toward the end wall.

3. Players may only be in possession of one noodle at a time, and all noodles must be thrown, not handed off, in level 1.

4. Noodles may not be touched or moved by hand if they are dropped in the playing area during level 1.

5. During level 1, only the Bucket Patrol may pick up their team's noodles off the ground and return them to their team's pile.

6. Level 2 does not begin until a team's entire pipeline is against the wall at the opposite end of the gym. Gator Skin balls, hockey sticks, and Frisbees may not be touched until level 1 is complete.

7. The pipeline may be directly handled during level 2. There may not be enough noodles to make one continuous pipeline from end line to end line. Sections of pipeline may be picked up and connected farther down the line once a ball has passed that section. Sliding the noodles along the floor to advance sections of pipeline is not allowed.

8. The first and last section of pipeline must be in contact with the end line before a ball can enter or exit the game.

9. Balls may not be touched or moved by hand during level 2. All balls must be placed on the pipeline and advanced down the pipeline using hockey sticks. Balls may not be carried down the pipeline. Players pushing balls may be in possession of only one stick.

10. In level 2, each pair of pipelines can be connected in any sequence or go in any direction.

11. Only the Bucket Patrol or players with hockey sticks may pick up any of their team's balls on the ground to return them to their team's hula hoop during level 2. Dropped balls may not be returned by hitting them along the ground.

12. Water shovels (Frisbees) must be used to scoop up the balls before dropping them into the water barrel.

13. Teams may not hinder each other. Each team is racing to complete both levels the fastest.

Variations

1. Eliminate level 2 for grades K through 1.

2. Divide the class into three or four teams if classes are extremely large and place one or two teams at each end of the gym. Teams follow the same procedures with the same amount of equipment, and if possible, are distinguished by the color of Gator Skin balls or pipeline they are using.

HEAD HONCHO II

Objective

This game allows students to practice honesty, fairness, and honorable sporting behavior. Derived from the game of Head Honcho (*No Standing Around In My Gym,* Human Kinetics), Head Honcho II is also a fast-paced and exciting game, requiring a little strategy, luck, and honesty. Ultimately, perseverance makes the difference.

Equipment

Needs are based on a class of at least 16 and no more than 80 students.

▸ 25-50 blindfolds, lummi sticks, or other items (blindfolds work well because they can be worn on different body parts instead of carried in the hands)

▸ 50-100 scarves, checkers, or other items (scarves work well because players can tie them to their body instead of carrying them in their hands)

▸ 5-gallon buckets (for the blindfolds and scarves)

▸ 100-200 tongue depressors or Popsicle sticks

▸ Floor tape to place on the ground inside each hula hoop helps eliminate confusion if any hoop is accidentally moved (optional)

▸ Hula hoops, carpet squares, or large poly spots (29)

Procedure

Before students arrive, set up all three levels. Place all hoops approximately 3 feet apart in a straight line in each row for all three levels. Note: Using like-color hoops will help students differentiate each row. For example, row 1 can have eight red hoops and row 2 can have 4 blue hoops. Set up five rows of hoops for level 1: eight hoops in row 1, four hoops in row 2, two hoops in row 3, two hoops in row 4, and one hoop in row 5. Place the bucket of sticks a few feet above row 5 in level 1. Set up five rows of hoops for level 2: three hoops in row 1, two hoops in row 2, and one hoop in rows 3, 4, and 5. Place the bucket of scarves a few feet above row 5 in level 2. Set up four rows containing one hoop each for level 3. Place the bucket of blindfolds a few feet above row 4 in level 3 (see diagram for setup).

The object of the game is for players to outwit their opponents (or have the best luck) in Rock, Paper, Scissors so that they can earn the most points. Before the game begins, demonstrate Rock, Paper, Scissors. Encourage players to play the game at the same rhythm. For example, players should show the symbol on the third count of 1, 2, 3. All players start in the first row of hoops in level 1 and advance one row every time they win a round of Rock, Paper, Scissors. Losers of a round must go back one row and find an empty hoop. The only exception is when there are more than 16 people in the game, in which case anyone losing in the first row in level 1 must go to the end of the line of those waiting to enter the game. The game moves at such a fast pace that players will never have to wait longer than a few seconds to get back in the game.

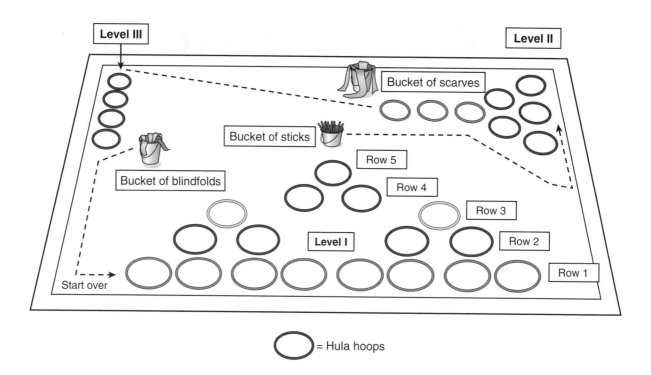

○ = Hula hoops

Players must advance through five rows in level 1 to earn a Popsicle stick and advance to level 2. There are also five rows in level 2 that a player must advance through to earn a scarf and move on to level 3. There are four rows in level 3 that a player must advance through to earn a blindfold before starting over at level 1. To earn a blindfold in level 3, a player must win Rock, Paper, Scissors four consecutive times. A loss in the third or fourth hoop results in going back to the first hoop in level 3 to start the level over.

As players collect items they must determine the best way to carry items while they continue playing Rock, Paper, Scissors. Players can earn multiple sticks, scarves, and blindfolds. Each item has the following point values: One stick equals 1 point, one scarf equals 5 points, and one blindfold equals 10 points. Players add up point values at the end of a 20- to 30-minute time limit or at the end of class. The player with the highest point value (not the most items collected) is declared the Supreme Head Honcho. Players with 31 to 50 points are declared Ultimate Head Honcho; players with 11 to 30 points are declared Awesome Head Honcho; and players with 1 to 10 points are declared Head Honcho. You may alter the point system as you see fit.

Rules and Safety

1. Winners of a round advance one row to an available hoop.
2. Losers of a round must go back one row to an available hoop. The only exception is when there are more than 16 people in a game, in which case anyone losing in the first row in level 1 must go to the end of the line of those waiting to enter the game.

3. Students not in one of the first eight hoops at the start of the game enter the game once any player advances from the first row.

4. Players waiting in a hoop may leave their hoop to face off against someone in another hoop in that same row. For example, if two players are waiting in the first row but are in different hoops, one player can quickly leave the hoop to join the other so play can continue.

5. All Rock, Paper, Scissors ties result in a do-over until someone wins.

6. Players winning in the fifth row of level 1 earn one stick. After retrieving a stick out of the bucket, players go to the beginning of level 2.

7. Players winning the fifth row of level 2 earn one scarf. After retrieving a scarf out of the bucket, players go to the beginning of level 3.

8. Any player losing in the first row of level 1 or 2 must go back to the last row of the previous level. For example, a player losing in the first row of level 3 must go back to the fifth row of level 2. However, a player losing in the first row of level 1 will not go back to the last hoop of level 3.

9. Players advancing through all four rows of level 3 without losing earn one blindfold out of the bucket before returning to level 1 to start over.

10. Players may have to wait a few seconds when advancing or going backward because the hoops may already be occupied. Simply have the players wait until a hoop is vacated.

11. Players often forget to go back a hoop when they lose because someone is usually ready to face off again right away.

12. Stop the game and total scores if there is no more of a particular item, and then start a new game.

13. The player with the most points at the end of the class is named the Supreme Head Honcho.

Variations

1. Eliminate levels 2 and 3 and play Head Honcho. The player with the most sticks at the end of the class is named the Ultimate Head Honcho.

2. Add more levels with different point values to increase the difficulty and length of the game.

3. Eliminate one or two rows from each level. This works best for smaller classes. Add more hoops to rows if particular areas are too congested.

HIDEOUT

Objective

This is a fast-paced aerobic game that focuses on the movement competencies of dodging and fleeing.

Equipment

Needs are based on a class of 48 students (4 teams of 11 players plus 4 Cops).

- Gymnastic mats or any equipment that can be used as a wall (4-8)
- Hula hoops (1 each in red, blue, yellow, green, and orange)
- Lummi sticks (12 each in red, blue, yellow, and green)
- Noodles cut in half (2-4 swim noodles cut in half or any other soft tagging instrument like foam paddles)
- Sonic Flag-A-Tag belts, any other detachable flag system, or juggling scarves (11 each in red, blue, yellow, and green)
- Traffic cones, 28-inch (4)

Procedure

Before students enter the gym, stack or stand the gymnastics mats in four different areas of the gym. These are team hideouts. Place one hula hoop behind each mat. Put the flag belts and lummi sticks of the same color inside each hoop (each hoop should have 11 flag belts and 12 lummi sticks of the same color). Place four cones in the four corners of the gym, place the remaining hoop in the center circle of the gym, and put the half-noodles inside the hoop (see diagram for setup).

Divide the class into four teams of 11 players. The remaining four players are Cops and should sit next to the hoop in the center circle, or Cop Precinct. Ask the rest of the students to put on their flag belts, sit in front of their team's hideout, and wait for further instructions.

The object of the game is to ransack the other team's hideouts and steal as much loot (sticks) as possible in the allotted time. Players achieve this by running to a hideout or the Cop Precinct in the middle of the gym, stealing one stick at a time and taking each stick back to their own team's hula hoop. If Cops tag players, the tagged players must give the Cops the stick so the Cops can take them to their precinct. Cops may only tag players who are carrying sticks.

Players must decide whether they want to try to steal loot from the other three teams or protect their own hoop containing their team's loot. Players can defend their hideout by pulling opponents' flags to keep them from stealing the loot. Players must immediately drop all flags they pull. Players with one or two flags on their belt can continue to participate. However, if a player loses both flags, that player must go to the nearest cone and run, jog, or walk a lap around the cones located in the corners of

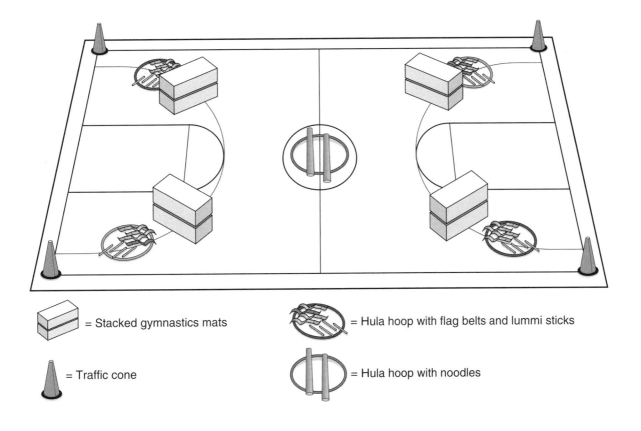

= Stacked gymnastics mats

= Traffic cone

= Hula hoop with flag belts and lummi sticks

= Hula hoop with noodles

the gym. After running one lap players find their flags, reattach them to their belt, and continue the game. The team with the most loot inside their team's hula hoop (including the Cops) at the end of the time limit (approximately 10-20 minutes) is declared the winner of that round. Reattach flags, return sticks, and begin a new round. Cops should trade their noodle for another player's flag belt to become part of that team for the next round.

Rules and Safety

1. Players and Cops may be in possession of no more than one stick at a time and must immediately take the stick to their own team's hoop.

2. Players who lose both flags must go to the nearest corner and run one lap around the cones.

3. Cops may only tag players with sticks and must take the stick to their hoop before they can tag other players. Cops may only tag one player at a time.

4. Players from each team can defend their hideout by pulling opponents' flags to keep them from stealing loot.

Variation

Eliminate the use of flags.

MED ALERT

Objective

Students work on cooperation, strategy, and teamwork in a game where speed is important but patience is the key to success.

Equipment

Needs are based on a class of 42 students (6 teams of 7 players).

- 5-gallon buckets or hula hoops (6)
- Frisbees, foam or regular (12)
- Hula hoops (1 each in red, blue, orange, green, purple, and yellow)
- Jerseys to designate teams (optional)
- Noodles cut in half (36; cut whole noodles in half to create half-noodles)
- Traffic cones, 28-inch (6)
- Wiffle, tennis, or hockey balls (49; number balls 1 through 7 with a permanent marker so that there are 7 of each number, unless 49 balls in 7 different colors are available)

Scenario

The Centers for Disease Control (CDC) has just been notified of a toxic virus spreading rampantly throughout seven jungle regions of the Congo. The CDC has created a vaccine and assigned the Special Forces Medical Alert Team to airlift the precious medicine to the seven treacherous drop zones of the Congo. It is a risky assignment, but with teamwork and determination, the Med Alert Team will save lives.

Procedure

Before students arrive, set out the buckets and traffic cones as depicted in the diagram. Place three hula hoops at each end of the gym and put seven like-numbered balls, six noodles, and two Frisbees inside each hula hoop (see diagram for setup).

The object of the game is for each team to successfully transfer one ball to each of the seven drop zones without touching the ball with any part of the body. Teams race against each other to determine who will accomplish this feat the fastest. No positions are assigned. Players are responsible for choosing what equipment to use and how they want to contribute to the game.

Divide the class into six teams and send each team to a hula hoop to sit down and await further instructions. Read the scenario to the class. The following solution is one example of how to win the game.

Two teammates each pick up a noodle from their hoop and place it on the ground or hold the noodles in the air waist high or higher, parallel with each other but side by side (see illustration below, left). Using the Frisbees, another teammate picks up or "sandwiches" a ball and places it on both noodles. After the ball is placed on the noodles, the teammates, without making any human contact with the ball, begin rolling the ball to the next pair of teammates holding a set of noodles, attempting to transfer the ball onto the next set. Teammates should maintain control of the ball with the assistance of the player with the Frisbees until the next set of noodles is ready for the transfer. Patience is the key! Teams continue this process to advance each of the seven balls from their team's hoop to all seven drop zones (six buckets and one cone). The traffic cones in the middle of the gym are each team's seventh and final destination. After arriving at a cone, each team must carefully and patiently set the ball on top of the cone (see illustration below, right). The first team to get one ball into each bucket and on top of one cone is declared the winner for that round. Clean up and start a new round.

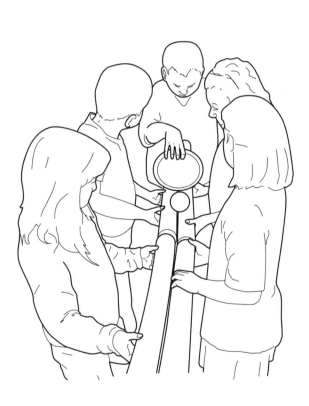

▶ *The beginning of the game: players start to move the ball down the noodles.*

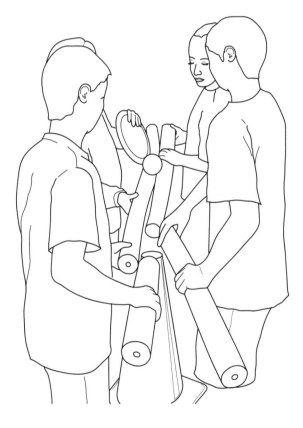

▶ *Players transfer the ball to the final drop zone: the cone in the middle of the gym.*

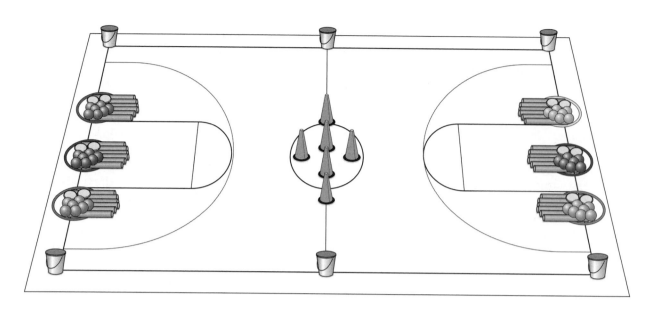

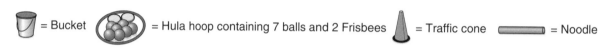
= Bucket   = Hula hoop containing 7 balls and 2 Frisbees   = Traffic cone   = Noodle

Rules and Safety

1. Players may not have more than one noodle in their possession, although multiple players may share the same noodle.
2. Only noodles and Frisbees may touch the balls. No human contact is allowed at any time. If human contact does occur, players must drop the ball and start again from where the ball was dropped.
3. Balls dropped from noodles must be picked up using Frisbees and started at the point where the ball was dropped.
4. Teams must begin from their hoop every time they start a new ball. Players may not advance toward any bucket while a ball is on any set of noodles.
5. Frisbees can be used to push or stop balls. Frisbees may not be used to carry or sandwich a ball down a set of noodles or catch a ball that falls off the noodles.
6. If cheating occurs, remove one ball from any bucket and return it to the cheating team's hoop.

Variations

1. Teams should always consist of 5, 7, or 9 players per group. Add a set of noodles or Frisbees depending on each group's size.
2. Increase game duration and difficulty by making teams return all dropped balls to their hoop before reentering them into the game.

NUCLEAR REACTION

Objective

Students must implement accuracy, teamwork, and quick decision making to save the city of Komodo by vaporizing the life-threatening nuclear reaction.

Equipment

Needs are based on a class of 48 students.

▶ Gator Skin balls (30-50)
▶ Hula hoops in different colors (40, with at least 5 of each color; for example 5 blue hoops creates one group or 10 orange hoops creates two groups of 5 players)
▶ Jerseys (8)
▶ Noodles (8 green and 8 orange, or whatever two colors are available)
▶ Traffic cones (8)

Scenario

The world's top undercover agents have flown to the heavily populated city of Komodo in the attempt to save its unsuspecting citizens from a nuclear radiation spill. It is only a matter of time before the radiation is hazardous enough to destroy all the city's inhabitants. The world's best agents must act fast to devise a plan to vaporize the deadly nuclear reaction.

Procedure

Spread out the hoops at one end of the gym and place all balls on the side opposite the hoops, preferably in the free throw area. Next, place all jerseys, traffic cones, and noodles in each of the four corners before classes arrive (see diagram for setup). Immediately upon arrival, instruct students to go sit on the side of the gym opposite the hula hoops. Read the scenario to the class.

The object of the game is to bond five electrons (5 like-color hoops connected and forming a circle) and surround one nucleus (any player without a hoop) to form a molecule. The nucleus is chosen only after the electrons have bonded. A complete molecule must then move as a connected team and obtain one item from each corner of the gym in order to vaporize the radiation. Give a demonstration of what a complete molecule looks like. Following is a sample illustration of one way for a molecule to be connected.

▶ *A complete molecule.*

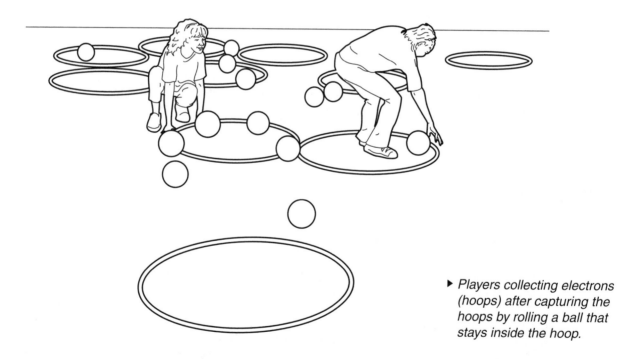

▶ *Players collecting electrons (hoops) after capturing the hoops by rolling a ball that stays inside the hoop.*

While remaining on the side of the gym opposite the hula hoops, all players start rolling or throwing balls to capture an electron (hoop) (see illustration). Players or teams may cross the midline at any time to retrieve up to five balls to bring back to their side. A player captures an electron by throwing or rolling a ball so that it stays inside a hoop. After capturing an electron, the player must immediately retrieve that color hoop, get inside it, and return to the other side of the gym.

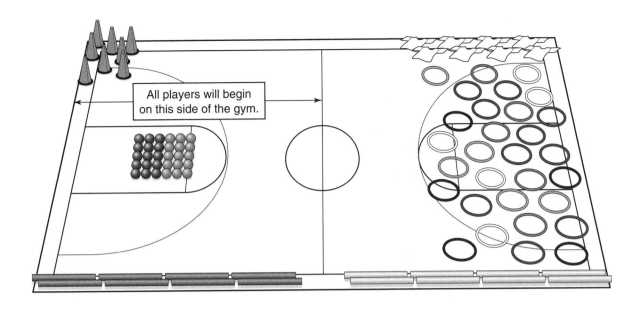

= Traffic cones   = Noodles   = Gator Skin balls   = Hula hoops   = Jerseys

After returning, the player must look for and connect with four other players with the same-color hoop. For example, a player who captured a blue hoop must get inside it, return to the other side of the gym, and connect with other players inside blue hoops. (Players connect by grabbing each other's hoop.) If there is only one other player inside a blue hoop, the player connects with that player until three more blue electrons are found. Remember, once electrons bond, they must stay connected and do everything together as a team.

While waiting to form a five-player molecule, a player or connected players should continue rolling balls to score them in any of their color of hoops. If the team is blue and they score a blue hoop, they can retrieve the hoop and give it to anyone without a hoop. A molecule is not complete until choosing a nucleus, which must be a player not currently inside a hoop. The completed molecule quickly travels to each corner of the gym and gathers one of each of the following items: a jersey for the nucleus to wear, a traffic cone for the nucleus to carry, and one noodle in each color to help bond the electrons.

When all items have been collected, the molecule goes to the center circle of the gym to vaporize the nuclear reaction. The vaporization process begins with the nucleus yelling a 20-second countdown by using the traffic cone as a megaphone. As the nucleus counts down, the electrons quickly revolve around the nucleus, vaporizing the nuclear radiation. The first team to successfully complete this process saves the people of Komodo and is declared the winner. Clean up and start a new round.

Rules and Safety

1. A ball must be inside a hoop to capture it. A player or connected players can capture more than one hoop and give it to any player without a hoop until the team reaches a total of five hoops. Remind each team that they can only capture hoops of their color.

2. Players must always remain inside their hoop. Connected players must always stay connected by holding each others' hoops when moving around or rolling balls to capture more hoops.

3. Any hoop is free game if it has a ball inside it and nobody claims it.

4. A team of five must choose any player without a hoop to be the nucleus before traveling to claim one item from each corner of the gym.

5. Play Rock, Paper, Scissors to settle disputes if two players think they captured the same hoop.

6. Players or teams may cross the midline to retrieve up to five balls to bring back and roll to capture more hoops.

Variations

1. To speed up the game, allow five electrons of any color to bond.

2. Instead of allowing players to cross the midline to retrieve balls, select 2, 3, or 4 players to be ball hounds and go to the side of the gym containing hula hoops. The ball hounds return all balls by rolling or throwing the balls to the other side of the gym. Pick new ball hounds for each round or allow them to switch positions with any players during the game.

3. Increase difficulty and duration of the game by using indoor Frisbees instead of balls.

4. If class size is small, modify the rules and equipment needs so that teams need only three or four electrons.

5. Allow defense by choosing one or two players to be radioactive viruses. Radioactive viruses can use a long noodle to knock away moving balls.

6. Increase the duration of the game by making players bowl or throw from behind the free throw line on the side opposite the hula hoops.

OPERATION "SPACE JUNKYARD"

Objective

This game uses teamwork, strategy, and critical thinking. Each team competes in Operation "Space Junkyard" in the effort to build a Gravity Glider and be the first to claim the one and only Golden Goblet.

Equipment

Needs are based on a class of 48 students (16 groups of 3 players).

- ▸ Blindfolds (16)
- ▸ Gator Skin balls (32)
- ▸ Hockey sticks (32)
- ▸ Hula hoops (16)
- ▸ Poly spots or paper plates (80)
- ▸ Scooters (16)
- ▸ Trophy (1)
- ▸ Additional hula hoops where teams can place their junk (1 per team; optional)

Scenario

The time for Operation "Space Junkyard" has finally arrived. It is a race held once every century for the universe's ultimate prize . . . the Golden Goblet! The galaxy's top space engineers will go head to head to see who comes out victorious. These space engineers will be tested like never before, but only one team will overcome seemingly impossible challenges to do what no human has ever done: build a spacecraft out of nothing but junk.

Procedure

Before students arrive, place eight stacks of five poly spots at each end of the gym. Next, place the blindfolds, hula hoops, scooters, Gator Skin balls, and hockey sticks against either sidewall in separate piles. Finally, place the trophy in the center of the gym. It is best to place the trophy on top of two stacked gymnastic mats (see diagram for setup). Instruct students to get into groups of three and go sit at a stack of hover spots (poly spots). Create one or two groups of four if there are students left and give these groups an additional poly spot.

The object of the game is to travel through the space junkyard (gym) by using the five hover spots, collecting glider parts to build a Gravity Glider that will enable the team to retrieve the Golden Goblet (trophy). Read the scenario to the class. Next, demonstrate how teams should use the five hover spots to travel through space. Players may not move anywhere unless they are on spots, so they must determine how to pick up

▶ *Gravity glider.*

and place the spots so that they can travel as a team to get to each glider part. Then demonstrate how all three team members must fly the Gravity Glider to hover and retrieve the Golden Goblet (see figure). Player 1 puts on the blindfold, stands on two poly spots (the other three poly spots can be discarded), and holds the hockey sticks behind him. Next, player 2 sits on the scooter and grabs the end of the hockey sticks. Then, player 3 stands inside the hoop and leans forward, grabbing the shoulders of player 2. Finally, all three players move the Gravity Glider as a single unit, making sure that player 1 goes in the right direction, player 2 does not let go of the hockey sticks, and player 3 does not let go of player 2's shoulders or allow the plutonium balls (Gator Skin balls) to roll out of the hoop.

Explain that in order to retrieve a part, players must collectively move on top of their five hover spots. Each team must strategize to figure out the quickest path to a glider part, try not to fall off the hover spots, retrieve the part, and return it to their team's home base. Once all seven glider parts have been collected, players may build their Gravity Glider and hover to the center. Communication is the key to success because teams must stay connected while guiding the blindfolded player to the Golden Goblet. The first team to retrieve the Golden Goblet is declared the winner for that round. Return all equipment and begin a new round.

Rules and Safety

1. Players must always be on a hover spot or they will fall into space. Players may not slide on the spots or share a spot with a teammate.
2. All three players on a team must move together on their hover spots when traveling to retrieve glider parts. Teams must also work together to return each glider part to their home base. Players may not throw glider parts.

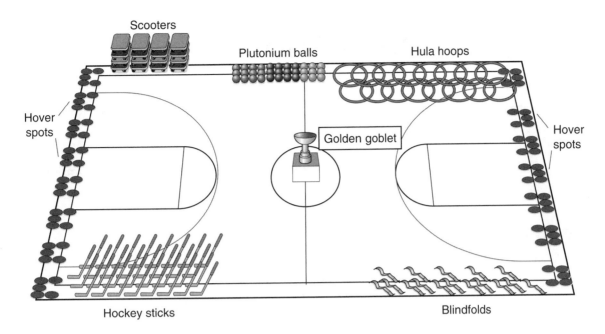

Scooters

Plutonium balls

Hula hoops

Hover spots

Golden goblet

Hover spots

Hockey sticks

Blindfolds

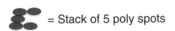 = Stack of 5 poly spots

3. Teams must attempt to travel in direct paths to each pile of glider parts.

4. Teams must return to home base and start over if any part of a player's body touches the floor or if a glider part is dropped while being transferred to home base. If a glider part is dropped, teams must return the part before starting over. Be lenient with those players whose feet are slightly bigger than the poly spot.

5. Only one glider part may be collected at a time. In some cases two of the same glider parts are necessary to build the Gravity Glider. Teams must return a second time to get the second glider part.

6. Only after all seven glider parts have been collected may a team build their Gravity Glider and go to the center of the gym to collect the Golden Goblet.

7. Once the Gravity Glider is built and the team travels to the Golden Goblet, the blindfolded player must be the first to touch the goblet.

Strategies

1. Teammates may grab one another's hands to avoid falling off a spot when reaching down to pick up spots.

2. Keep spots close together to prevent falling.

Variations

1. Allow teams to branch off to collect glider parts if you play with groups of four or more.

2. Allow teams to carry all the glider parts at once without having to return items one at a time to home base.

PACEMAKER

Objective

This outrageously aerobic game introduces the concept of pacing and its importance in physical activity. It is also a great way to reinforce locomotor skills.

Equipment

Needs are based on a class of 75 students (5 teams of 15 players).

- ▶ 5-gallon buckets (10; 5 empty and 5 with Popsicle sticks)
- ▶ 1000 tongue depressors or Popsicle sticks (200 per bucket)
- ▶ Hula hoops or poly spots (9 each in green, orange, blue, red, and yellow; like-color hoops or spots are recommended, but not required. Poly spots are recommended for larger classes because they take up less space)
- ▶ Pacemaker Progressions posters (5; taping the lists on the wall is recommended), page 69
- ▶ Traffic cones for separating teams (optional)

Procedure

Before students arrive, place five rows of 9 like-color hula hoops on the floor. Place an empty bucket along with one list at the beginning of each row of hoops. Finally, place a bucket of sticks at the end of each row (see diagram for setup).

The object of the game is for each team to pace themselves and earn the most sticks within the 20- to 30-minute time limit. Divide the class into five teams and assign each team to a different row. Explain that the verb *pace* means to be careful not to move or exercise too quickly so that you do not get too tired to finish. For example, long distance runners will run at a steady rate of speed for the entire race. If they run too fast then they may get too tired to finish the race. Pace is the key to completing the Pacemaker Progressions list (page 69) without having to quit due to exhaustion. Reading "The Tortoise and the Hare," especially with younger students, may enhance student comprehension of the concept of pace.

On your signal, players look at their Pacemaker Progressions list and begin performing as a team the first locomotor movement. For example, players read the first movement on the list, "Jump on both feet," and begin jumping until they cross the end line at the opposite end of the gym. Upon completing the skill, players each retrieve one stick from their bucket. The first player to cross the end line and collect a stick gets into the first hula hoop. The next teammate to collect a stick jumps into the first hoop and taps the first player's back to "bump" the first player to the second hoop. (Give a brief demonstration of bumping before the game begins; see illustration.) Bumping continues throughout the game, resulting in a constant rotation of players through the 10 hoops. Only one player may occupy a hoop at a time, and players cannot advance until someone taps their back (see diagram for the flow of the game).

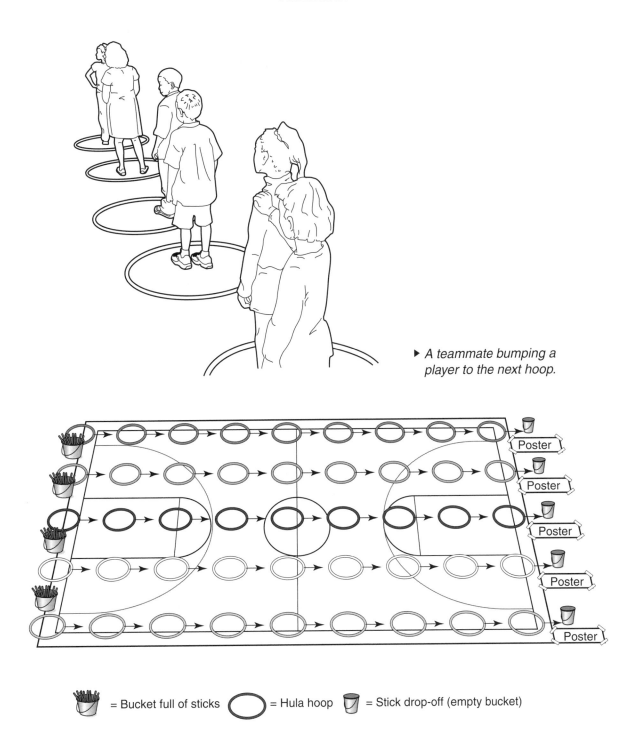

▶ *A teammate bumping a player to the next hoop.*

![= Bucket full of sticks] = Bucket full of sticks ![= Hula hoop] = Hula hoop ![= Stick drop-off] = Stick drop-off (empty bucket)

Players getting bumped from the last hoop must drop their stick into their team's stick drop-off (bucket at the end of the row) before reading the Pacemaker Progressions list to find out the next locomotor skill. Players must do their best to follow the progression of locomotor skills on the list. Although most players won't notice, the faster players will eventually pass some of the slower players. It is possible that slower players will skip some skills, especially when a teammate asks them to do a partner skill even though the slower player has not yet completed some of the previous skills. This is acceptable because the underlying objective of the game is aerobic exercise and participation. The team who earns the most sticks within the designated time limit is declared the winner. Return all sticks and start a new game.

Take opportunities before, during, and after the game to point out examples of how players are and are not demonstrating pacing. Emphasize that the players who pace themselves do not necessarily go as fast but are able to last longer and attempt more locomotor skills without getting exhausted.

Rules and Safety

1. Players should attempt to follow the progression of locomotor skills on the Pacemaker Progressions list.
2. Only one player may occupy a hoop at a time.
3. Players may only advance one hoop after being bumped. Players must remember that they cannot advance until someone taps their back.
4. Each player may take only one stick out of the bucket upon the completion of each locomotor skill.
5. Players must carry their stick and drop it in their team's bucket after being bumped out of the last hoop.

Variations

1. Eliminate 2, 3, or 4 hoops per row or eliminate one row of 10 hoops for classes with more than 30 but fewer than 50 students. Too many hoops may cause some players to get stuck in hoops for a long period of time.
2. Larger classes may need additional rows, especially if there appear to be "traffic jams" of players waiting to get into the first hoop.
3. Add easier or more difficult locomotor skills to the Pacemaker Progressions list.
4. Add various objects that must be carried in a certain way. For example, have students balance a beanbag on the back of their hand, balance a tennis ball on a badminton racket, or perform different scooter skills.
5. Allow players to keep their sticks and determine the top five players at the end of a round.
6. Play boys against girls: Who has the best average (number of sticks divided by the number of girls or boys in the class)?

Pacemaker Progressions

Complete the list in the following order. Start over if you complete the entire list. Remember to *pace* yourself!

Make sure you get a stick each time you travel the length of the gym.

1. Jump on both feet
2. Skip
3. Hop on one foot
4. Gallop
5. Crab walk
6. Sprint
7. Bear crawl (crawl, allowing only your hands and feet to touch the floor)
8. Slide step (galloping sideways)
9. Hopscotch (straddle jump, hop, straddle jump, hop)
10. Lock elbows and hop on one foot with a partner
11. Walk back to back sideways with a partner
12. Carefully piggyback a partner
13. Lock elbows and skip with a partner
14. Free choice (pick your favorite and do it again)

Great job—now start over!

From *PE2theMax: Maximize Skills, Participation, Teamwork, and Fun* by J.D. Hughes, 2005, Champaign, IL: Human Kinetics.

PINDEMONIUM

Objective

This is a game where pandemonium, throwing and bowling for accuracy, and teamwork can actually coexist.

Equipment

Needs are based on a class of 60 students.

- ▸ Basketball goals (2)
- ▸ Bowling pins (50-100; the more the better)
- ▸ Gator Skin balls or soft foam balls (50-100; the more the better)
- ▸ Indoor Frisbees (25-50; optional)
- ▸ Jerseys, red and blue (5 of each color)
- ▸ Trash cans, 32-gallon (4; these are only needed if using indoor Frisbees)

Procedure

Before students arrive, set up bowling pins behind each end line of the gym, slightly in front of the end wall. Place all Gator Skin balls and Frisbees in the center circle. Next, place a trash can at the corner of each end line and sideline (see diagram for setup). Separate the class into two teams, one team at each end line. Select five players from each team to be goalies and instruct them to put on the jerseys on their side of the gym.

The object of the game is to roll balls or throw Frisbees in an attempt to knock all of the opposing team's bowling pins over. All players not wearing jerseys begin rolling balls or throwing Frisbees from their side of the gym, attempting to knock down the opposing team's bowling pins. All balls must be bowled, not thrown! No one is allowed to play defense and no one is allowed in the goalie box except for the goalies. While remaining in the goalie box (the area between end line and wall), goalies block balls and Frisbees, guarding their team's pins. Goalies must retrieve balls and Frisbees to provide their teammates with ammunition since teammates are not allowed past the end line.

Players also have the option of earning a 10-second reward for their team. A 10-second reward allows the team's goalies 10 seconds to reset the pins that have been knocked down. Players can only earn 10-second rewards by throwing a Frisbee inside one of the opposing team's trash cans or by scoring a basket in the opposing team's basketball goal. Players who score baskets or get Frisbees in trash cans immediately yell "Score." You can ask to make sure a basket was scored or check the trash can and then start a 10-second countdown. As soon as the countdown starts, the goalies of the scoring side reset their pins while everyone else continues playing the game. Goalies must stop setting up pins at the count of 0. A winner is declared when all of a team's pins get knocked down. If this doesn't happen, whichever team has the most pins standing after a predetermined time limit (approximately 10-20 minutes) is the winner. Instruct teams to reset the pins and have goalies pick a player to take their spot before starting a new round.

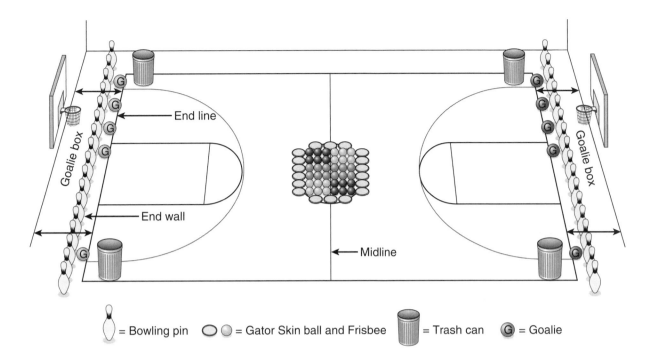

= Bowling pin ⬭ ⬭ = Gator Skin ball and Frisbee 🗑 = Trash can Ⓖ = Goalie

Rules and Safety

1. Players must stay on their side of the gym and may not cross over the midline.
2. No throwing overhand or throwing at players.
3. Goalies must remain within the goalie box. At no time may teammates without jerseys enter the goalie box.
4. Once a pin is down, it stays down unless a 10-second reward is earned.
5. Ten-second rewards can only be earned when a Frisbee lands inside one of the opposing team's trash cans or a basket is scored with a Gator Skin ball in the opposing team's basketball goal.
6. Only the goalies of the scoring side may reset their pins during a 10-second reward.
7. The game does not stop during a 10-second reward.
8. Balls and Frisbees can be ricocheted off the walls in order to knock over pins.
9. No kicking the balls!
10. The teacher may knock over pins for any rule violations.

Variations

1. Players must throw Frisbees through standing targets instead of into trash cans.
2. Allow players to roll or throw Gator Skin balls.

SCOOTER BLITZ

Objective

This is an exciting scooter game that focuses on teamwork, offensive and defensive strategy, and rolling and throwing skills.

Equipment

Needs are based on a class of 48 students.

- Bowling pins (40-60; the more pins, the longer the game)
- Gator Skin balls (30-40)
- Scooters (40)
- Jerseys to distinguish each team or just the goalies (optional)
- Traffic cones, 28-inch (6-10 per side)

Procedure

Place all of the Gator Skin balls inside the center circle. Line up the traffic cones 7 to 10 feet from the end line and set up the pins near each end wall. Finally, place an equal number of scooters at both ends of the gym (see diagram for setup). When students arrive, separate players into two teams and instruct players to get a scooter. Have teams sit with their scooters at opposite end lines. The players that do not get scooters are the goalies for the first round. Instruct goalies to get inside their team's goalie box (the area between the traffic cones and end wall).

The object of the game is to roll or throw balls in an attempt to knock all of the opposing team's bowling pins over. Scooter players may move anywhere within the scooter zone (all of the space between both sets of traffic cones) as they roll or throw balls to knock over the opposing team's pins. Encourage students to think of and implement strategies to knock down pins. For example, teammates can save all balls and then charge the other team, bombarding them with lots of balls. It's easier to defend a few balls as opposed to a whole lot of balls. Scooter players may not enter the goalie boxes. Scooter players may choose to play offense, defense, or a combination of both positions at any time during the game. Offensive players may carry one ball at a time and attempt to knock over the opposing team's pins. **Hint:** Ricochet balls off the walls or roll them between the goalies' feet to knock over pins. Defensive players may position their scooter or hold their hands up to block balls being rolled and thrown by their opponents. Making contact with other players and stealing balls are both illegal.

Goalies may not exit the goalie box but may defend their pins by knocking away balls that enter the goalie box. Goalies can move anywhere within the goalie box as long as they remain in front of their pins. Goalies can use their bodies to make a human wall as long as their feet do not go past the end line.

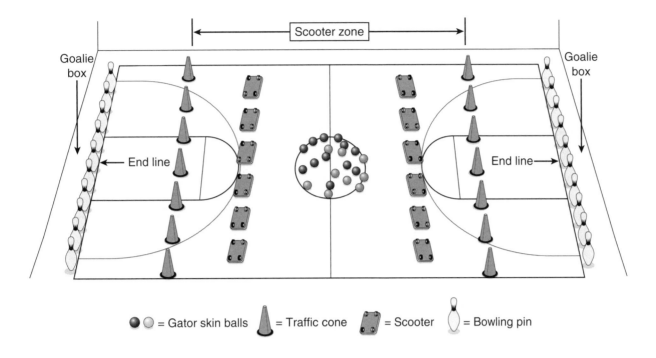

●○ = Gator skin balls   ▲ = Traffic cone   ▢ = Scooter   ♙ = Bowling pin

A winner is declared once all pins on one side are knocked over. If this doesn't occur, whoever has the most pins standing after 15-30 minutes is the winner. Start a new round by instructing the goalies to switch with someone from their team and having everyone else set up the pins and return the balls to the center.

Rules and Safety

1. Scooter players can roll or throw balls while remaining seated on their scooter. No throwing balls at players or kicking balls!

2. A player may be in possession of one ball at a time.

3. Once a pin is down, it stays down.

4. Scooter players may play offense or defense. Stealing balls or making contact with the opposing team are both illegal.

5. To get past human walls, balls can be played off actual walls.

6. Goalies can roll or throw balls out of the goalie box to teammates or they can use the balls to attempt to knock over the other team's pins.

7. Goalies may not exit the goalie box and scooter players may not enter the goalie box.

8. The teacher may knock over pins for rule violations.

SHOCKEY

Objective

This game incorporates teamwork, strategy, critical thinking, and most important, persistence, in a shocking new way to play with hockey sticks.

Equipment

Needs are based on a class of 50 students.

▶ Gator Skin balls, 4- to 7-inch (15-30 red and 15-30 blue; assign each team multiple colors if there are not enough red and blue, such as red and orange for one team and blue and green for the other)

▶ Hockey sticks (46)

▶ Jerseys (4 red and 4 blue, or whatever colors are available)

▶ Lummi sticks or short-handled hockey sticks (4)

▶ Trash cans, barrels, or boxes (4)

Procedure

Before students arrive, place 23 hockey sticks, 2 lummi sticks, and 4 jerseys at each end of the gym and 1 trash can at the corner of each end line. Next, place all Gator Skin balls inside the center circle (see diagram for setup). When students arrive, select four players from each team to put on a jersey and get either a lummi stick or hockey stick. Divide the remainder of the class into two teams and send them to opposite ends of the gym to get hockey sticks, sit down, and wait for further instructions. Explain that not everybody has the same equipment because there are different positions in the game, but teammates may trade positions during a game or before the next round.

The object of the game is for players to capture as many of their team's Gator Skin balls as possible within the 15- to 35-minute time limit. Explain that each team has three positions and that players may choose to be Scorers, Bashers, or Sweepers. Scorers, or players with hockey sticks, work in groups of two or more in order to capture (pick up) and carry balls using the blade of the hockey stick, attempting to score them in their team's trash cans. Challenge players to think of the best ways to carry balls with the blade of the stick (see illustration for one possibility). Bashers, or players who have jerseys and lummi sticks, attempt to bash (knock off) the balls that the opposing team's Scorers are carrying (see second illustration). A bashed ball must be picked up by the Basher and returned to the center circle before the Basher can attempt to bash any other balls. Sweepers, or players with jerseys and hockey sticks, sweep (hit away) the opposing team's Gator Skin balls that are on the ground; in other words, the Sweepers play keep-away with the opposing team's Scorers.

Scorers for each team begin capturing the Gator Skin balls in their team's color, attempting to avoid Bashers and Sweepers as they try to score the balls in their team's trash cans. You may pause the game at your discretion and ask the Bashers and Sweep-

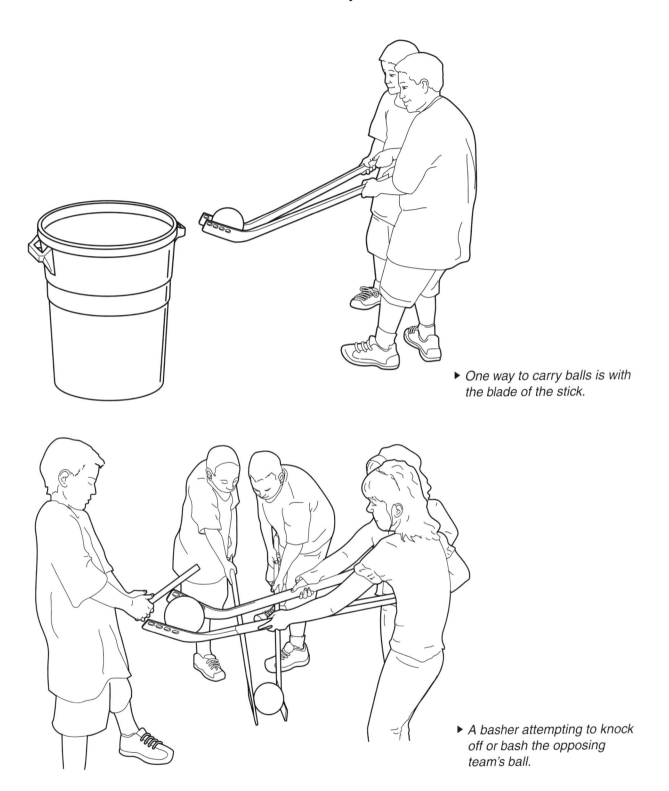

▸ *One way to carry balls is with the blade of the stick.*

▸ *A basher attempting to knock off or bash the opposing team's ball.*

ers to switch positions, or you may wait and have players switch positions just before starting a new round. Encourage teams to never give up, because patience will be tested due to the difficulty of getting the balls past Bashers and Sweepers. The team who scores all the balls in their team's color first or scores the most balls within the time limit established by the teacher is declared the winner of that round. Clean up and start a new round.

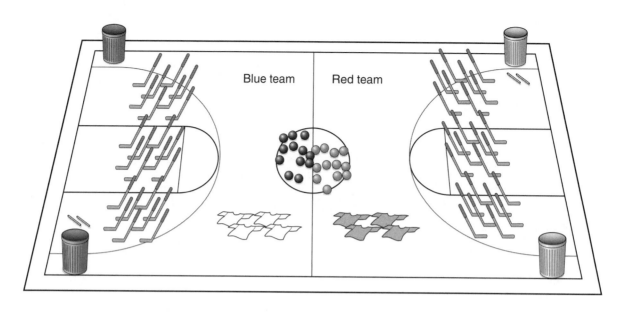

/ = Hockey stick   ▯ = Trash can   ● ○ = Gator Skin balls   \\ = Lummi sticks   ▱ = Jerseys

Rules and Safety

1. No high sticking! High sticking is when the blade of the stick goes above the knee on the backswing or follow-through. All high sticking results in a time-out for the first offense and loss of stick for the second offense.

2. Sweepers may only sweep away balls that are on the ground.

3. Scorers must use sticks to carry the Gator Skin balls while working in groups of two or more. If scorers drop a ball, they may quickly pick it up. Players cannot make human contact with the balls and cannot hit the balls to advance them down the court or keep them away from a Sweeper.

4. Scorers may not touch a teammate's stick.

5. Balls scored in the trash cans cannot be removed. Trash cans cannot be moved or tipped over.

6. Scorers may not touch the other team's Gator Skin balls.

7. Bashers may only bash one ball at a time and the ball must clearly be off the ground. The Basher must return each bashed ball to the center circle.

Variations

1. Bashers must use their lummi stick to hit a ball to the center circle before they can bash another ball.

2. If high sticking becomes a problem, make Sweepers use their feet to sweep balls away.

3. Add more Bashers and Sweepers to the game to increase difficulty.

SUPER BOWL

Objective

This crazy, erratic game reinforces bowling for accuracy.

Equipment

Needs are based on a class of 60 students.

- ▶ Bowling pins (40; enough for two-thirds of the class)
- ▶ Gator Skin balls (50-100)
- ▶ Jerseys to designate teams (optional)
- ▶ Tennis ball (1)
- ▶ Traffic cones (17)

Procedure

Before students arrive, spread the Gator Skin balls randomly around the gym. Place half of the bowling pins on each sideline of the gym. Then put one traffic cone with a tennis ball on top in the center of the gym. Finally, divide the gym into three sections using the traffic cones (see diagram for setup).

When the class arrives, divide students into three teams. Instruct players on teams 1 and 3 to each get one bowling pin and set it up on their sideline and then sit against the wall and await further instructions. Instruct team 2 to gather anywhere in the middle of the gym, have a seat, and await further instructions.

The object of the game is to knock down the opposing team's bowling pins by rolling balls at the pins. To begin the game, all teams start rolling balls at the opposing team's pins. Players may only be in possession of one ball at a time. Teams 1 and 3 are the outside teams. These players must stand behind their pins and may only retrieve balls that are located between their sideline and the wall. Players on teams 1 and 3 may use their hands to knock away balls that are coming toward their pins or may roll balls to deflect oncoming balls. They also roll balls at the opposing team's pins. Players may only guard the pin they are standing behind. After their pin is down, players continue to roll balls at the opposing team's pins. Once a pin is down, it stays down, even if it was accidentally knocked over.

Team 2 is the middle team and has no bowling pins. Team 2 is against teams 1 and 3 and may roll balls at either team's pins. Team 2 has the advantage of traveling anywhere within the basketball court boundaries to retrieve balls. Although team 2 players can go almost anywhere to get a ball, they cannot roll balls until they are clearly within the middle section between the lines of traffic cones. Team 2 is also responsible for guarding the re-setter cone (cone and tennis ball), located in the center of the gym. Two players, without touching the cone, may guard the re-setter cone by blocking any oncoming balls. Teams 1 and 3 have a chance to win a single 10-second countdown by knocking the tennis ball off the cone. This 10-second countdown, performed by the

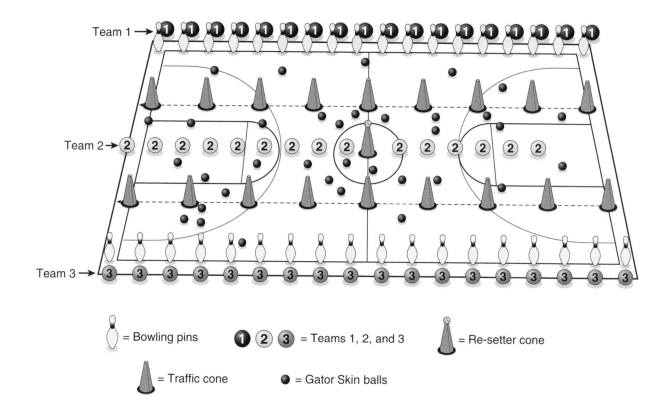

Team 1 →

Team 2 →

Team 3 →

⚲ = Bowling pins   **1** **2** **3** = Teams 1, 2, and 3   ◭ = Re-setter cone

▲ = Traffic cone   ● = Gator Skin balls

teacher, allows teams 1 and 3 a one-time opportunity to reset all downed pins. Team 2 players continue play during the 10-second countdown. The re-setter pin is not reset once it has been destroyed.

The team with the most pins standing when the time elapses (usually 5 to 10 minutes) is declared the winner for that round. If all pins are downed before the time expires, the middle team is declared the winner of that round. Teams rotate upon completion of a round. For example, team 1 moves to the middle section, team 2 moves to team 3's space, and team 3 walks across the gym to team 1's original space. This rotation continues after each round so that all teams occupy each section at least once.

Rules and Safety

1. Balls must be bowled underhanded.

2. A player may be in possession of only one ball at a time.

3. Players on teams 1 and 3 must stand behind their pin and may not enter the basketball court. They must come up with strategies to defend their pin since they can't touch the pin itself.

4. Once a pin is down, it stays down unless the re-setter cone is destroyed. If destroyed, a 10-second countdown is awarded to allow the outside teams a one-time opportunity to reset all downed pins.

5. Players on team 2 can go anywhere within the basketball court boundaries to retrieve balls but must return to their section before rolling a ball.

Variations

1. Add more re-setter cones to the middle section so that there are more opportunities to reset pins.

2. Give each outside player two pins to guard or allow players to help guard a teammate's pin.

3. Allow an outside team to retrieve balls if all of their pins are down and the re-setter cone has already been destroyed. Outside players must get back behind their line before rolling the balls.

SUPREMACY

Objective

In this game, hockey dribbling and shooting for accuracy are essential in order to capture the General and gain supremacy.

Equipment

Needs are based on a class of 60 students.

- 5-gallon buckets (6)
- Bowling pins, white or like-color (40-60), different colors (2; use colored tape to distinguish both pins from the other pins if colored pins are unavailable)
- Gator Skin and/or yarn balls or foam balls, 3- to 5-inch (75 or more), 8-inch or larger Gator Skin balls (12)
- Hockey sticks (48)
- Jerseys (10 in two different colors, such as 5 green, 5 orange)
- Tennis balls (4)
- Traffic cones, 18- to 28-inch (22)
- Additional traffic cones or poly spots for marking the dotted line depicted in the setup diagram (optional)

Scenario

A special ops team consisting of the world's top spies and explosives engineers has been assembled to travel into enemy territory. Their mission is to disarm enemy land mines, capture the General, and return home to negotiate a successful peace plan.

Procedure

Before students arrive, place 24 hockey sticks, 20 to 30 bowling pins, three buckets, six large Gator Skin balls, and five jerseys inside the free throw area in each half of the gym. Place all yarn balls and small Gator Skin balls in the center of the gym. Then place five traffic cones around one colored pin (the General) behind each free throw area. If possible, set up poly spots or traffic cones to help students visualize the imaginary line depicted in the diagram. Finally, place two traffic cones with tennis balls on them at each side of each end (see diagram for setup).

The object of the game is to disarm the enemy's force field, destroy their land mines, and capture their General. Divide the class into two teams and assign each team to one end of the gym. Select five players from each team to be the Defenders. The Defenders put on a jersey and get a hockey stick. Instruct all other players to either get a hockey stick (Explosives Engineers), a bucket (Ammo Patrol), or two large Gator Skin balls

(Spies) before sitting down to await further instructions. All players are responsible for performing the duties of one of four positions. The position a player is responsible for is based on the equipment that he or she possesses. Read the scenario to the class.

Briefly explain the four positions:

1. Explosives Engineers use their hockey stick to dribble the small Gator Skin balls and yarn balls and then hit them in the attempt to disarm the enemy's land mines (knock down bowling pins).

2. The Ammo Patrol carries buckets and gathers ammunition to supply teammates.

3. Spies carry the two large Gator Skin balls and bowl the balls to disarm force fields (knock tennis balls off the opposing team's two cones) and destroy land mines.

4. Defenders wear jerseys and protect land mines with their hockey stick.

Provide a 20-second countdown to allow each team to set up their bowling pins anywhere on their side of the gym. Remind players that pins cannot be placed directly next to each other or behind anything. On your signal, each team's Explosives Engineers begin to disarm the land mines by knocking down the opposing team's bowling pins. Because each team's midline is protected by an invisible force field, Explosives Engineers cannot cross the midline until the opposing team's force field has been disarmed. The two disarming devices (traffic cones with tennis balls) located inside each team's minefield activate each team's force field. This force field is disarmed by hitting the cones with Gator Skin or yarn balls until the tennis balls are knocked off. Once the force field is disarmed, Explosives Engineers may cross the midline but may only go as far as the free throw line (designated on the diagram by dotted lines and cones) as they continue attacking and destroying the land mines. The closer the Explosives Engineers get, the better their chance of destroying the remaining land mines. The General can only be captured after all of the land mines have been destroyed. The General may get knocked down before all of the land mines have been destroyed. Teams are allowed to reset the General each time the General is prematurely destroyed.

The Ammo Patrol carries buckets and may go anywhere in the gym to gather ammunition to bring back to teammates. The Ammo Patrol's job is crucial—since the Explosives Engineers are not allowed in the area from the free throw line to the wall, they cannot retrieve ammunition where most of it gets stuck.

Spies carry large Gator Skin balls and bowl the balls to disarm force fields, destroy land mines, and ultimately capture the General. Spies are extremely important to their team because they have bigger balls, which make it much easier to destroy the opposition's targets. Spies can move anywhere within the gym to gather no more than two large Gator Skin balls at a time before returning to their side to roll the balls. The spies will be eliminated from the game if they are caught knocking pins over while traveling through the opposing team's side.

Defenders may only protect land mines by blocking balls with their feet and hockey sticks. Defenders may not physically stand in front of a land mine, but they may place their stick in front of it. Also, a defender may not guard more than one pin at a time. Defenders may not guard the General or the disarming devices. Defenders may reset the General if it is knocked over before all of the land mines are destroyed. Defenders perform the duties of the Explosives Engineers when there are no longer any pins to guard. For example, if two bowling pins remain, then only two Defenders may stay and guard those pins and all other Defenders become Explosives Engineers.

Explosives Engineers and Spies may attack and capture a team's General once all land mines have been destroyed. Immediately after knocking the "General" pin down, players capture the General by getting the pin and holding it up high to declare victory.

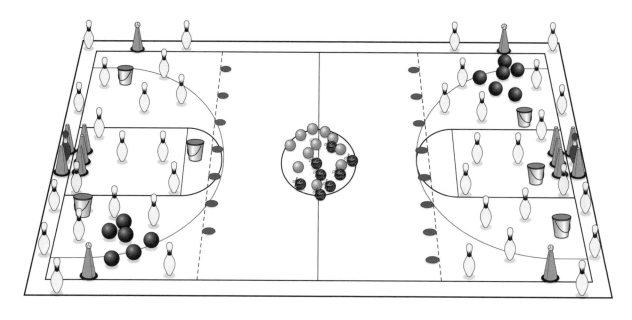

A winner is declared when the General has fallen and no land mines remain. You may also allow players to bring the General to their side once the General has fallen. Reset the pins, return all balls to the center, have players switch positions, and start a new game.

Rules and Safety

1. Absolutely no high sticking! High sticking is when the blade of the stick goes above the knee on the backswing or follow-through. High stickers will receive penalty time based on the severity of the infraction. Some examples of penalty time can include being placed in time out in a penalty box or not being allowed in a position where hockey sticks are used.

2. A player's body or stick may not cross the boundary lines when hitting or rolling balls.

3. Land mines (bowling pins) or disarming devices (cones with tennis balls) may not be reset when destroyed, even if accidentally destroyed. The only exception is if the General is knocked over before all of the land mines are destroyed.

4. Spies may have two balls at a time and may travel anywhere to retrieve balls. Spies may roll or bowl balls, but may not throw balls.

5. Defenders are the only players allowed within the boundaries of the free throw line and wall on their team's side. Defenders remain Defenders as long as there is a pin for them to guard.

6. Each Defender may only guard one pin at a time. Defenders may not stand directly in front of a pin, but they may place their stick in front of the pin. The teacher may knock over any pin that is being protected by more than one Defender.

7. The General cannot be captured until all land mines have been destroyed.

Variations

1. Give each team one Reactivator pin. The Reactivator pin should be placed somewhere within the minefield. This pin is surrounded by cones like the General, but when it is destroyed the destroying team gets a 20-second countdown to "reactivate" or reset their destroyed land mines. The Reactivator pin may only be destroyed once.

2. Use hockey balls or pucks instead of Gator Skin balls. Please note that due to the nature of this game, students are at a greater risk of being hurt if hit in the feet and shins with the hard balls or pucks.

3. Eliminate the use of hockey sticks if enough sticks are not available or too much high sticking is occurring. Instead have players bowl Gator Skin balls to destroy the land mines.

4. Allow Spies to throw the large Gator Skin balls.

UNDER SIEGE

Objective

This is an intense cardiovascular game where offensive and defensive strategies are crucial for placing the castles under siege and seizing the crown and jewels.

Equipment

Needs are based on a class of 48 students.

- ▸ Gator Skin balls (1 blue, 1 red, 1 yellow, and 1 green)
- ▸ Hula hoops (1 blue, 1 red, 1 yellow, and 1 green)
- ▸ Sonic Flag-A-Tag or Velcro flag belts (2 flags per belt), or the Rip Flag System (3 flags per belt) or juggling scarves (2 scarves at the hip) may be substituted (12 each in blue, red, yellow, and green)

Procedure

Before students arrive, place a hula hoop in each corner of the gym. Inside each hoop, place the like-color Gator Skin ball and the 12 like-color flag belts.

When classes arrive, instruct students to put on any color of flag belt, sit down beside the hoop that is the same color as their flag belt, and await further instructions. Explain that the players on the same side of the play area are on the same team. For example, if the blue and red colors are on the same side, then they are against yellow and green players on the other side of the play area. Note: The game can be set up with two teams of the same color on each side if enough like-color flag belts are available. For example, one side can have two teams of blue and the other side can have two teams of green. The original equipment needs were established to prepare for extremely large classes because combining color teams requires fewer like-color flag belts of each of the four colors.

The object of the game is to be the first team to steal the other side's Gator Skin balls (crown and jewels) and place them in their team's hula hoops. Players may choose to play offense or defense at any time during the game. The offensive strategy involves running (or whatever locomotor movement you predetermine) and attempting to pull flags from both teams on the opposite side of the play area. After pulling a flag, players immediately drop it to the ground. Remind students that they are not only trying to pull the opposing team's flags, they are also trying to avoid opponents who are trying to pull their flags. The defensive strategy involves players staying near their team's hula hoop (castle) to guard their crown and jewels (see illustration). Combined colors on the same team may help guard each other's crown and jewels. For example, red players may guard red and blue crowns and jewels and blue players may guard blue and red crowns and jewels. Defenders may stop players from attacking the castle by pulling their flag. Play continues until both of a player's flags have been pulled. Players who lose both flags must find two flags in their color and return to their hoop to put them on before reentering the game.

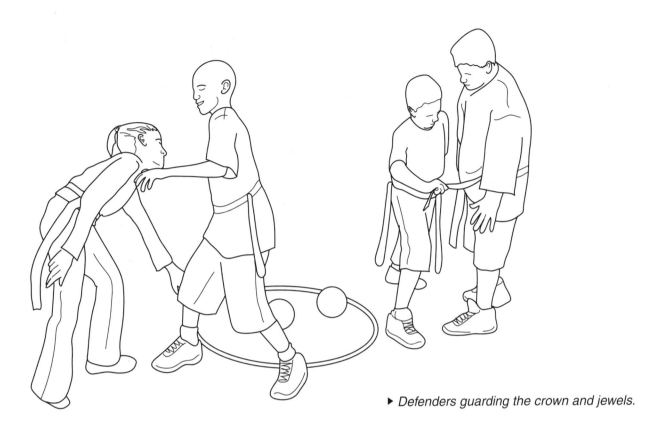

▶ *Defenders guarding the crown and jewels.*

Help students realize that they must incorporate strategies to lure defenders away from their castles so their team can steal the Gator Skin balls. Players must adhere to the following rules once a Gator Skin ball has been captured:

1. Players must drop a captured ball when their second flag is pulled.

2. A ball automatically goes to the opposing team when it is dropped. For example, a red player who steals a ball and gets both flags pulled must drop the ball for a yellow or green player to pick up and return to their castle. When attempting to return the ball, if the yellow or green player gets his flags pulled, that player must drop the ball for a red or blue player to retrieve. This process can easily go back and forth until the ball is finally returned or captured.

3. A captured ball that has made it into an opposing team's hoop cannot be removed.

A round is over when one side has stolen all of the opposing team's balls and returned them to either of their own hula hoops. Start a new round after everyone has located and reconnected their flags and returned the Gator Skin balls to their like-color hoop.

Rules and Safety

1. Players may not protect or hide flags. Belts must clearly display flags.

2. Defenders must stand outside of the hoop to guard the crown and jewels.

3. A player may be in possession of one ball at a time and may not pass the ball to a teammate.

4. A captured ball must be dropped if the player in possession of the ball gets both flags pulled. Players may not tackle, grab arms, or pull clothes to get flags.

5. When a ball is dropped, it automatically goes to the opposing team.

6. Players who lose both flags must retrieve their flags from the ground and return to their like-color castle (hoop), get inside the hoop, and reattach both flags before reentering the game.

7. Players who have lost both flags may not pull the opposing players' flags until they have reattached their own flags.

8. A captured ball that has made it into an opposing team's hoop cannot be removed.

9. A team wins once it has both of the opposing team's balls inside either of its own hoops.

Variations

1. Eliminate two colors and play color against color. This works well for classes of 40 or less.

2. Add more Gator Skin balls for each team to protect. Gator Skin balls may be substituted with other items such as footballs, beanbags, lummi sticks, and so on.

3. Allow teams to recapture balls as many times as possible. This variation increases the game's duration.

4. Increase difficulty and cardiovascular endurance by increasing the size of the play area (for example, consider playing the game outside on a large field).

WELL DESIGNED

Objective

This game challenges each team to work together to create a well-designed "body" of items.

Equipment

Needs are based on a class of 42 students (6 teams of 7 players).

- Badminton rackets (6)
- Basketball (1)
- Bowling pins (6)
- Frisbees (6)
- Hockey sticks (6)
- Hula hoop (1)
- Jump ropes (7)
- Laminated Diagram 1 and 2 (6), see pages 91 and 92
- Lummi stick (1)
- Noodles (6)
- Pencils (6)
- Playground ball (1)
- Poly spots (6)
- Scooter boards, 12- or 16-inch (8)
- Scooters, 12-inch (6)
- Traffic cones, 28-inch (6)
- Well Designed Fitness Checklist (6), see page 90
- Yarn balls (6)

Procedure

Before students arrive, place all badminton rackets, bowling pins, swim noodles, Frisbees, hockey sticks, jump ropes, poly spots, scooters, traffic cones, and yarn balls in the center of the gym. Next, place the lummi stick, hula hoop, jump rope, basketball, playground ball, and scooters along the sidelines of the gym, separate from each other (see diagram). Place all six copies of diagram 1 (page 91) on a stage or secluded area so that no teams will see them until fulfilling the requirements of the Well Designed Fitness Checklist (page 90). Diagram 2 (page 92) is for round 2, or it can be used instead of diagram 1. Instruct students to form groups of six or eight. Send each group to any area in the gym, where they select one group leader. Instruct each group leader to get a pencil and Well Designed Fitness Checklist from you.

The object of the game is to be the first group to complete the fitness activities on the checklist in order to collect all 10 items and put them together in the arrangement depicted in diagram 1.

To play the game, students follow this procedure:

1. Perform 1 of the 10 activities from the Well Designed Fitness Checklist. The leader of each group is responsible for the checklist and for each team's compliance with the rules.

2. Once a fitness activity has been completed, the leader checks off that activity. (Hint: Some activities take longer to complete than others. Based on the available equipment, only one group at a time will be able to perform certain activities. It would be wise for teams to determine which activities they will have to take turns with and which activities take longer and then complete those activities first so that they will not waste time waiting for another team to finish them.)

3. The leader then selects one teammate (a different person each time) to get an item from the center and bring it back to the group.

4. The group continues performing the activities, one at a time, until all fitness activities have been completed and all 10 items collected.

5. One player then runs to the stage and looks at diagram 1. The player reports back to the team to tell them about the diagram and lay out the placement of each of the 10 items. The diagram may not be brought back to the group. To clarify understanding, different players may go one at a time to review the picture and report any necessary changes. Continue this process until the team agrees that what is displayed out on the floor exactly reflects the picture in the diagram.

6. The teacher is called over once a team is in agreement and believes their picture is ready. After looking at a copy of the diagram, the teacher responds with either a "Yes" or "No" (subtle hints may be provided to help correct minor mistakes). "No" means that a team must figure out and correct what is incorrectly positioned.

7. The first team to receive a "Yes" is declared the winner of that round. If time permits, instruct students to return all items to the center while you switch diagram 1 with diagram 2. Round 2 is played just like round 1, but it may be shortened by allowing teams to keep their items from round 1, omitting procedures 1 through 4.

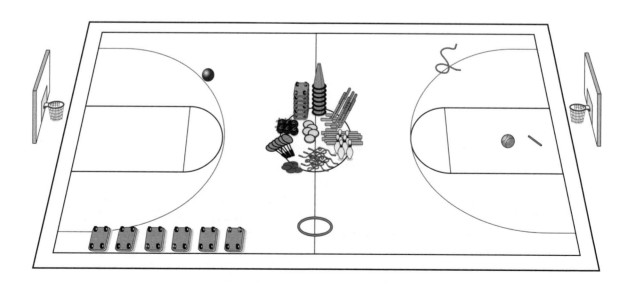

Rules and Safety

1. The leaders of each group are responsible for making sure no one cheats and all activities are successfully completed.

2. Only one fitness activity from the checklist can be performed at a time. It is up to the teacher to determine whether a team should redo an activity for doing it incorrectly.

3. One item may be taken from the center once an activity has successfully been completed. All 10 activities must be completed and all 10 items collected before a team can see the diagram.

4. One person from each team may go look at the diagram, but diagrams may not be brought back to the group. Players also may not yell changes back to their team or stand in a place where they can compare the diagram to their display. A different player from the team must go look at the diagram each time it needs to be reviewed. Continue this process until the team agrees that what is displayed on the floor exactly reflects the picture in the diagram.

5. A "No" from the teacher means that a team must go back and correct what is incorrectly positioned.

Variations

1. If a team has an uneven number of players, allow one player to skip an activity. For example, if all teams have five players except for one team, which has six, then one player from the six-player team sits out so that only five players complete the activity. A different player sits out of each activity.

2. Create new diagrams based on available equipment.

3. Modify the fitness checklist by adding or omitting activities to meet your classroom objectives.

Well Designed Fitness Checklist

To earn an item from the center, everyone on your team must perform all 10 activities. Go on to another activity or wait until a group is done if an activity is occupied. The activities may be performed in any order, but only one activity may be performed at a time. Ask the teacher for a demonstration or explanation if your group does not understand exactly how to perform an activity.

Place a check (✓) next to an activity when it has been completed. Your team cannot repeat an activity to earn an item.

___ Activity 1: Circle up and perform "Ring Around the Rosie" one time (sing it out loud).

___ Activity 2: Perform 10 jumps each with the jump rope (take turns).

___ Activity 3: Sit on the scooters and once connected (holding hands, locking arms, grabbing the scooter handles), make one lap around the gym, staying close to the wall.

___ Activity 4: Perform the game Circle the Circle (from *No Standing Around in My Gym,* pp. 44-45, published by Human Kinetics) by holding hands and forming a circle with the hoop around two of the player's connected hands. Transfer the hoop (2 times), without letting go of any hands, from person to person until it goes completely around the circle.

___ Activity 5: Walk one lap backward around the gym while holding hands. Your team must start over if anyone's hands come unlocked. Stay close to the wall.

___ Activity 6: Line up and perform an "over and under" pass with the playground ball. Player A passes the ball over his head to B and B passes the ball under his legs to C and so on until the ball reaches the last person. The last person runs to the front to start the process over. Continue this process until the first person who started the game ends up back in the front of the line.

___ Activity 7: Jog two laps around the gym as a team, staying close to the wall.

___ Activity 8: Perform 30 jumping jacks together as a team, counting each one out loud.

___ Activity 9: Each person in your group must shoot the ball until they make a basket.

___ Activity 10: While holding the lummi stick, a player must jog one lap around the gym and then hand the stick off to the next teammate until everyone has jogged a lap. Stay close to the wall.

From *PE2theMax: Maximize Skills, Participation, Teamwork, and Fun* by J.D. Hughes, 2005, Champaign, IL: Human Kinetics.

Well Designed Diagram 1

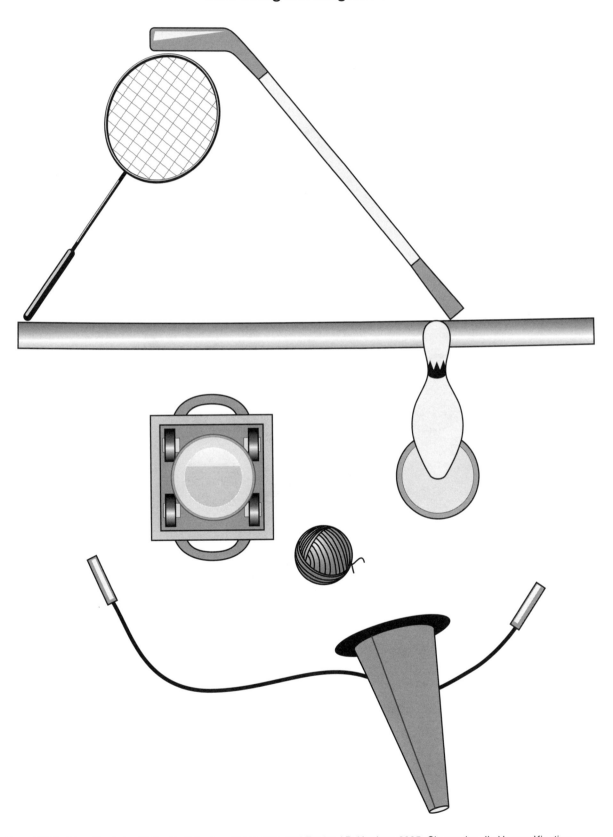

From *PE2theMax: Maximize Skills, Participation, Teamwork, and Fun* by J.D. Hughes, 2005, Champaign, IL: Human Kinetics.

Well Designed Diagram 2

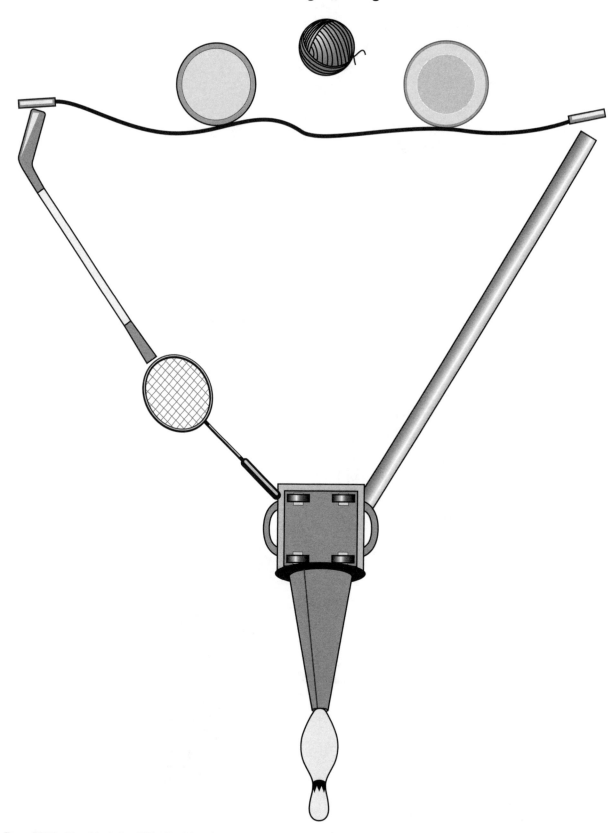

From *PE2theMax: Maximize Skills, Participation, Teamwork, and Fun* by J.D. Hughes, 2005, Champaign, IL: Human Kinetics.

WHEEL 'N DEAL

Objective

This is a fast-paced game where teamwork, decisiveness, and communication skills are critical to wheel 'n deal teams to success.

Equipment

Needs are based on a class of 60 students (12 teams of 5 players).

▸ Hula hoops (13)
▸ 13 different items, preferably objects that are small and of the same color: red and black checkers, scarves, green and blue lummi sticks, birdies, Wiffle balls, orange and purple beanbags, yellow and blue yarn balls, blindfolds, and foam Frisbees (13 of each item; substitute other items if necessary)
▸ Add or subtract hoop(s) and items depending on the number of teams. There should be one more hoop and set of items than teams.

Procedure

Before students arrive, set out the 13 hula hoops as depicted in the diagram. Next, place one of each of the 13 items inside each hula hoop (see diagram for setup). When students arrive, instruct them to get into groups of five, go sit beside one of the hula hoops except for the center hoop, and await further instruction.

Explain that each team is on a wheel 'n deal shopping spree. Make students aware that there are 13 different items inside their team's hula hoop. The object of the game is to be the first team to collect all 13 of a single item. Players from each team must decide who will be Scouts, who will be Traders, and which item the team wants to collect. Scouts take items from their team's hoop to seek out and wheel 'n deal with other teams for their particular item (see illustration). Traders hang out at their team's trading post (hula hoop) and wheel 'n deal their items with Scouts from other teams. The General Store (hula hoop located in the center of the gym) is available for all players to go and trade one of their items for any item in the store. Students exchange items on their own since nobody is stationed at the General Store.

Play begins with each team determining which of the items they want to collect. Take this time to mention that there are only 13 of each item, so teams should choose wisely. Also at this time, teams should decide who will be Scouts and Traders. It is up to each team to decide how many Scouts or Traders they want to use. For example, some teams may choose not to have Traders, although it is highly recommended to have at least one Trader to make sure items are not traded from their hoop without permission.

Scouts take one item and quickly venture out to wheel 'n deal at other teams' trading posts for items that their team needs. Once a trade occurs, Scouts return the item to their team's hoop and continue the game. In some cases Scouts will not get exactly

▶ *Wheeling and dealing.*

what they are looking for or will come across a Trader who is unwilling to wheel 'n deal. In this case the Scouts may need to wheel 'n deal with other teams until they have the particular item necessary to make a trade with the unwilling party. Encourage students to be friendly with one another because this type of wheeling 'n dealing takes persistence and patience.

You may need to demonstrate an example of this type of trade, especially with the younger grades. For example, say team A wants a red checker from team B, but team B will only trade for a scarf. In order to make the trade, team A must find a scarf from their team's hoop or trade another team for a scarf before trading with team B for a checker.

Traders can refuse to trade any items they possess. All 13 items cannot be collected unless teams are willing to wheel 'n deal the 13 items in their possession, and there is a good chance that some teams will be collecting the same item. It is up to the individual teams to decide whether or not to keep their original item or begin wheeling 'n dealing for a new item. The team to persevere and get all 13 items first or the team to get the most items within the time limit is declared the winner of that round.

Before starting a new round, take a few minutes to reequip each hoop with the 13 different items, or, while still following the same rules, make a game out of the cleanup

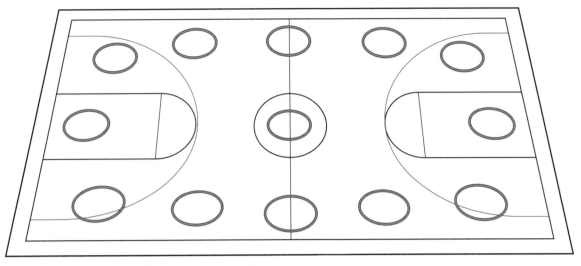

Objects in each hula hoop:

- = Red checker
- = Scarf
- = Green lummi stick
- = Birdie
- = Wiffle ball
- = Orange beanbag
- = Yellow yarn ball
- = Blindfold
- = Foam Frisbee

- = Black checker
- = Blue lummi stick
- = Purple beanbag
- = Blue yarn ball

to see which team can get all 13 different items in their hoop the fastest. Start a new round once everyone and the General Store have 13 different items.

Rules and Safety

1. Each player may only take one item at a time to wheel 'n deal for another item.
2. Wheeling 'n dealing always involves an exchange of one item for another, whether it is with another team or at the General Store. Cheating has occurred if a team has less than or more than 13 items. In this case, pause the game, resolve the matter, and remind players of the rule.
3. All trades must take place at a hoop. Traders can refuse to trade any items they possess.
4. Teams may decide to collect a new item if they determine that another team is collecting the same item. No team has to change, but the teams will eventually lose if they are unwilling to change items.
5. A trade cannot be made at an unoccupied team's hoop.
6. Throwing items is not allowed!

Variations

1. Increase the difficulty by adding more teams with fewer players. In this game description there were 12 teams with 5 players collecting 13 items. If you create 3 more teams without increasing players, there would be 4 players per team (15 teams total) collecting 16 items. Remember, if there are 15 teams, then there now must be 16 different items (one item for each of the 15 teams and one item for the General Store).

2. Speed up the game by requiring teams to collect only 7, 8, and so on of the 13 available items in order to win a round.

3. Use multiple items. For example, instruct teams to collect two different items, seven of one item and six of the other item.

4. Increase difficulty and duration by making players perform locomotor movements other than running as they go around wheeling 'n dealing.

YEAH, BABY!

Objective

Students will learn how to strategically place items to avoid losing them to the other team, work on finesse, and improve throwing for accuracy.

Equipment

Needs are based on a class of at least 20 but no more than 80 players.

- ▸ 5-gallon buckets (10)
- ▸ Basketball goals at opposite ends of gym, set 8 feet high (2)
- ▸ Bowling pins (20)
- ▸ Gator Skin balls (40-50)
- ▸ Hula hoops (20)
- ▸ Indoor Frisbees (40-50)
- ▸ Jerseys (6 in two different colors, such as 3 green, 3 orange)
- ▸ Traffic cones (10; any size works well)
- ▸ Wiffle, tennis, or hockey balls (10)

Procedure

Before students arrive, place half of all hula hoops, bowling pins, buckets, cones with balls on them, and jerseys at each end of the gym. Place Frisbees and Gator Skin balls in the center circle (see diagram for setup).

The object of the game is to capture and retain more items than the other team. Divide the class into two teams and instruct teams to go to opposite ends of the gym. Select three captains from each team and have them put on a jersey.

Each team has one minute to strategize and determine the best place to put items so that they are as hard to capture as possible. Yell "Go!" once the minute is up. Each team begins throwing Frisbees or bowling balls, attempting to capture items from the other team. An item is captured once a thrown Frisbee or bowled ball 1) lands and stays inside of a hula hoop or bucket, 2) scores a basketball goal, or 3) knocks down a bowling pin or knocks a ball off a cone. Players who capture items yell "Yeah baby!" to let others know of their accomplishment before they cross the midline to retrieve the captured bucket or hula hoop. When a basketball goal is made, players are allowed to retrieve three items to bring back to their side. Captured items can be placed anywhere a player chooses, but they may not be picked up and moved once they have been placed on the ground.

Captains, or defenders, are the only players allowed to protect their team's items by blocking with their bodies or by throwing Frisbees and balls at thrown objects. Captains may not touch or move items to better locations, but they may instruct teammates

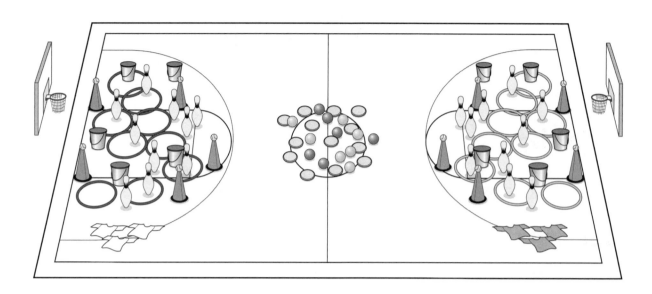

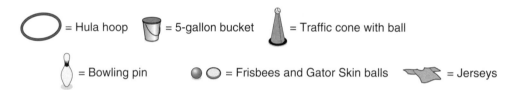

where to put recently captured items. Captains can also participate in the game like everyone else.

The team to capture the most items within the time limit, about 10 to 20 minutes, is declared the winner for that round. Return all items and start a new round.

Rules and Safety

1. Only the jersey-wearing captains are allowed to play defense. All other players must clearly be attempting to capture items. The teacher may take away defenders if their team commits any rule violations.

2. Only one ball or Frisbee may be handled at a time.

3. Players may capture one item at time (or three items for making a basketball goal) to bring back to their side. Both the ball and cone must be carried over if they are captured. No one may help a player retrieve captured items.

4. Balls or Frisbees cannot be removed from inside items until they are claimed. Any players may cross the midline and retrieve unclaimed items that their team has captured.

5. Captured items can be placed anywhere a player chooses, but they may not be moved once they have been placed on the ground. Items may not be stacked on top of each other or in corners.

6. Defenders may protect their team's items by blocking with their bodies or by throwing Frisbees and balls at thrown objects. Defenders may not touch or move items to better locations, but they may instruct teammates where to put recently captured items.

7. Defenders may switch with their teammates any time during the game by giving their jersey to whomever they choose.

8. Players are not allowed to physically knock over other items when retrieving captured items from the side of the opposing team. If they accidentally knock down pins or balls, the other team will be allowed to reset those items.

Variations

1. Add more items to be captured.

2. Create new ways to capture items.

3. Assign different point values to each item and tally results at the end of the game.

4. Make players travel using different locomotor movements.

5. The teacher may want to place items closer for grades K through 1 to make the game less difficult.

Suggested Readings and References

Cavert, C., and S. Sikes. 2002. *50 more ways to use your noodle.* Tulsa: Learning Unlimited Corporation.

Chen, A., and P.W. Darst. 1999. *Confirming situational interest in physical activity: Testing the theoretical construct in a middle school participatory setting.* American Educational Research Association 1999 Conference Proceedings, 33. Montreal, Canada.

Gallahue, D., and F. Cleland-Donnelly. 2003. *Physical education for all children.* Champaign, IL: Human Kinetics.

Graham, G. 2001. *Teaching children physical education.* 2nd ed. Champaign, IL: Human Kinetics.

Lawler, P. 2002. Gym class isn't just dodgeball anymore. *U.S. News and World Report,* June 3, 50-52.

LeFevre, D. 2002. *Best new games.* Champaign, IL: Human Kinetics.

Maina, M.P., M. Griffin, and K. McCurdy. 2002. Critical thinking simplified: A five-step approach to teaching how to solve problems in physical education. *The GAHPERD Journal* 35(2): 17-19.

National Association for Sport and Physical Education (NASPE). 2004. *Moving into the future: National standards for physical education.* 2nd ed. New York: McGraw-Hill.

National Association for Sport and Physical Education (NASPE). 2004. *Physical best activity guide: Elementary level.* 2nd ed. Champaign, IL: Human Kinetics.

Weir, T. 2000. New PE "life" sports are emphasized instead of the team concept so that no child is left out. *USA Today,* May. www.healthfirstusa.com/education/usatoday.html.

Young, J. 2003. Does your PE meet today's needs? *Principal Magazine,* January/February v. 82 no. 3: 26-30. www.naspe.org/comm/p01-02-03.htm.

About the Author

J.D. Hughes, MA, has received numerous awards throughout his teaching career, including the Georgia Elementary Physical Education Teacher of the Year for 2004 and an honorable mention in USA TODAY's 2003 All-USA Teacher Team program (he was the only PE teacher to be so honored that year). Hughes was certified in 2001 by the National Board for Teaching Professional Standards, and he received a specialist's degree in education in 1999. He is currently elementary physical education chair for the Georgia Association for Health, Physical Education, Recreation and Dance. A member of the advisory board for PE Central's Best Practices and Grades 3-5 Lesson Plans, he also presents at workshops and conferences. He enjoys spending time with his wife, Beth, and daughters, Janie and Josie, as well as cycling, weight training, and NASCAR racing. J.D. invites you to contact him via e-mail at pe2themax@bellsouth.net. He welcomes any questions or comments you might have about *PE2theMAX,* including purchasing additional copies and requesting workshop information.

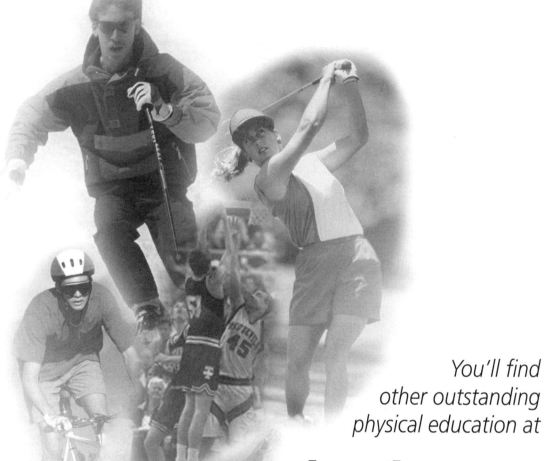